Social Skills Groups
for Children and Adolescents
with Asperger's Syndrome

A Step-by-Step Program

Kim Kiker Painter

Jessica Kingsley Publishers
London and Philadelphia

First published in 2006
by Jessica Kingsley Publishers
116 Pentonville Road
London N1 9JB, UK
and
400 Market Street, Suite 400
Philadelphia, PA 19106, USA

www.jkp.com

Library of Congress Cataloging in Publication Data
Painter, Kim Kiker (Kimberly Kiker), 1977-
    Social skills groups for children and adolescents with Asperger's syndrome : a step-by-step program / Kim Kiker Painter.
        p. cm.
    Includes bibliographical references and index.
    ISBN-13: 978-1-84310-821-4 (pbk. : alk. paper)
    ISBN-10: 1-84310-821-6 (pbk. : alk. paper) 1. Asperger's syndrome--Patients--Rehabilitation. 2. Asperger's syndrome--Social aspects. 3. Social skills in children. I. Title.
    RJ506.A9P24 2006
    618.92'858832--dc22

                        2006000871

British Library Cataloguing in Publication Data
A CIP catalogue record for this book is available from the British Library

ISBN 978 1 84310 821 4

Printed and bound in the United States by
Integrated Book Technology, Troy, New York

Contents

PART III: FURTHER READING

Acknowledgements

First and foremost, I would like to thank my graduate school advisor, Lee A. Rosén, Ph.D., who has provided me with the encouragement, direction, and insight needed to successfully complete this book. Dr. Rosén has not only been vital in the completion of this project, but also in my development as a clinician, an assessor, a consultant, and a person. He has provided me with numerous opportunities to work with children, adolescents, and families in various settings—opportunities which have proven invaluable. As is Dr. Rosén's nature, he went above and beyond standard expectations; not only did he provide me with countless training opportunities, he also took the time to mentor me. Dr. Rosén's guidance, expertise, and humor throughout my graduate work have helped me become a better clinician, student, researcher, and person and I thank him for the time he has invested in me.

I would also like to thank Karla J. Gingerich, Ph.D., for her expertise in the area of autism spectrum disorders. Dr. Gingerich supervised the social skills groups of which I was a part, and her knowledge of individuals with Asperger's Syndrome is impressively extensive. I appreciate her sharing her expertise with me, as it has been essential in the creation of this book.

On a more personal note, I would like to thank my friends and family who have provided support, motivation, and encouragement to me throughout the writing of this resource. I owe many thanks to my husband, Todd, who has lovingly endured days of writing, editing, and grumpiness. He has been an ever constant source of comfort, perspective, and humor and I am so grateful to have him in my life.

Introduction

This resource is intended specifically to assist clinicians and teachers in treating individuals with Asperger's Syndrome (AS) in a group setting. It has evolved over the past several years and stems from the social skills groups that many graduate students led at Colorado State University (CSU). I consider myself very fortunate to have been a part of leading these groups. Their existence began when Lee A. Rosén, Ph.D., the director of the Psychological Services Center (PSC) at CSU, received a call from a parent of a child with AS, asking if there were any social skills groups in the community to treat children with AS. When Dr. Rosén explained to her that there were no such groups in the area, she suggested that he should start one. Dr. Rosén asked one of his graduate students to lead a group, and other students were also interested. Dr. Rosén arranged for Karla J. Gingerich, Ph.D., to supervise these groups, as her area of expertise is in working with individuals with autism spectrum disorders (ASDs).

Ever since that first phone call, the groups have been running at PSC. Dr. Rosén has played a pivotal role both in starting the groups and in assuring that they have continued. He has encouraged other graduate students to become involved and has also provided supervision for the groups. In addition, Dr. Rosén has facilitated the "passing of the torch" from graduate student to graduate student as they have completed their studies and left CSU.

Dr. Gingerich supervised the social skills groups for the first few years of their existence and shared her expertise of individuals with ASDs with the graduate students leading the groups. Her supervision was vital to their early success, as when they were first formed, little research existed to guide the curriculum. With Dr. Gingerich's expertise and the "round table" discussions among group leaders in supervision, the activities for the groups formed.

In addition, many of the activities that formed the group sessions came from parent concerns reported to therapists. For example, one parent commented that her son always had difficulty on holidays because he would (rudely) comment after opening a present that he did not like the gift. Through brainstorming sessions within supervision, the idea of a "goofy gift exchange" arose.

Thus, the clients and families who have participated in the social skills groups at PSC deserve many thanks in the development of this resource. Both the children and parents who were involved directly taught our staff about the specific needs and learning styles of individuals with AS and helped shape this resource.

Many other graduate students gave generously of their time and expertise to help facilitate the groups that served as the starting point for this resource, including: Sylvia

Acosta, Brandi Chew, Bob Johnson, Jennifer Lindner, Tracy Richards, Laurie Schleper, and Gail White.

While the topics presented in this resource are empirically grounded, the development of the specific activities for each topic was heavily influenced by the social skills groups at PSC. There is very little empirical literature that outlines the exact activities used to teach specific social skills. Therefore, it is clear that others may have used similar activities to the ones presented here. The purpose of this resource, however, is to provide an empirically grounded program that combines research and practice to form a "ready to use" curriculum.

The biggest challenge for children and adolescents with (AS) is knowing how to interact with others in a social setting. In fact, the key deficit in children with AS is in social skills (Krasny *et al.* 2003). These children lack the basic social skills that most children develop naturally as they mature. While it is well known that these children need specific treatment to help them be more successful socially, clinicians and teachers have struggled to find resources to help guide them. There are a number of resources available that address social skills problems in general but very few have been developed to address specifically the needs of children with AS. An empirically grounded treatment program is presented here to guide clinicians and teachers as they strive to treat individuals with AS effectively.

PART I

ASPERGER'S SYNDROME AND SOCIAL SKILLS

1. Overview of Asperger's Syndrome

The key deficit in Asperger's Syndrome

The key deficit found in children and adolescents with Asperger's Syndrome (AS) is their lack of social skills. They do not know or use the basic social skills that come more naturally to other people (Krasny *et al.* 2003). They often do not have a full appreciation of the social "rules" of interaction. For example, they do not understand the give-and-take nature of conversations and find it difficult to figure out how others are feeling (Hauck *et al.* 1995; Klin, Volkmar, and Sparrow 2000). Children and adolescents with AS often have problems making and keeping friends, and if they have friendships, these relationships may be strained (Attwood 2000). Because social skills are foundational to almost all relationships, business as well as personal, individuals with AS often find it challenging to succeed (Marriage, Gordon, and Brand 1995).

What is Asperger's Syndrome?

AS is a psychological disorder that falls under the umbrella of autism spectrum disorders (ASDs) (Smith, Magyar, and Arnold-Saritepe 2002). The deficits that these children show are thought of as falling on a broad continuum. Disorders on the autism spectrum include: AS, high-functioning autism (HFA), pervasive developmental disorder–not otherwise specified (PDD-NOS), and autism—highlighting the wide range of skills and abilities these individuals may have (Tsai 2000). AS generally falls at the higher functioning end of the spectrum.

AS is a lifelong condition that affects both children and adults (Njardvik, Matson, and Cherry 1999). The primary feature of AS is significant difficulty engaging in age appropriate, reciprocal social interactions (American Psychiatric Association [APA] 2000; Attwood 2000, 2003). Essentially, people with AS do not understand the basic premise of social interactions—that they are reciprocal in nature. In other words, they struggle with showing interest in what others are saying, knowing when to talk and when to listen, and responding appropriately to both the body language and statements of another person. Having good social skills is absolutely vital to successful interactions with others regardless of the setting, and as a result, individuals with AS experience difficulties in a number of areas of their lives (Marriage *et al.* 1995).

Although AS is usually diagnosed in childhood, individuals generally struggle with the symptoms throughout their lives (APA 2000; Njardvik *et al.* 1999). Someone with AS can certainly learn social skills and improve their functioning in the world, but they will probably continue to have difficulty with social interactions, especially those that are more complex (e.g., dating).

A brief history

Asperger and Kanner

Asperger's Syndrome is named after Hans Asperger, born in 1906 in Vienna. In 1938, Asperger coined the term "autistic psychopathy" to describe the children with whom he worked (Felder 2000). Asperger's second doctoral thesis was entitled "'Autistic Psychopathy' in Childhood" and was published in 1944. This influential paper served as the foundation of what is now called Asperger's Syndrome (Frith 1991; Wing 1998). The common current belief is that the children Asperger described were high-functioning children on the autism spectrum and thus the label "Asperger's Syndrome" has been used in reference to such children.

Although AS is usually associated with Hans Asperger, another luminary, Leo Kanner, described a group of children that appeared to be much like the children Asperger described. Kanner was born in 1896 in Austria and coined the term "early infantile autism". He published his paper on early infantile autism in 1943, one year before Asperger's paper on autistic psychopathy (Frith 1991; Wing 1998). Both Asperger and Kanner used words like "autistic" and "autism" to describe the lack of social integration these children demonstrated (Wing 1998). They are heralded as pioneers in recognizing autism as a developmental disorder and not merely a "childhood affliction."

Recognition of Asperger's Syndrome as a disorder

The World Health Organization's *International Classification of Diseases, 10th Edition* (*ICD-10*) included AS for the first time as a subdivision of the pervasive developmental disorders. The criteria used for AS at that time were: a lack of "significant" delay in language and cognitive development, social impairments, and stereotyped behaviors and interests (Wing 1991). AS appeared in the *Diagnostic and Statistical Manual of Mental Disorders, 4th Edition* (*DSM-IV*) for the first time in 1994 under the larger category of pervasive developmental disorders (Wing 1998). Both the *ICD-10* and *DSM-IV* pointed to impairments in social interaction, stereotyped behaviors, and peculiar areas of interest (Wing 1998).

2. Diagnostic and Assessment Issues

Diagnostic criteria

The most recent edition of the *Diagnostic and Statistical Manual of Mental Disorders*, the *DSM-IV-Text Revised* (APA 2000) outlines specific criteria for diagnosing Asperger's Syndrome (AS). Others (Gillberg and Gillberg 1989; Szatmari, Brenner and Nagy 1989) have also created diagnostic criteria for AS, but the most widely used are those in the *DSM-IV-TR* (Ghaziuddin, Tsai and Ghaziuddin 1992).

The *DSM-IV-TR* classifies AS as a pervasive developmental disorder (PDD), which also includes other disorders such as autistic disorder, Rett's disorder, and childhood disintegrative disorder (APA 2000). Children with PDDs experience severe deficits in social skills, communication skills, or display stereotyped interests, movements, or activities. PDDs are usually identified early in life and many children with PDDs also have mental retardation. Yet children with AS do not, by definition, have delays in cognitive development (APA 2000).

Clinical manifestations

SOCIAL SKILLS DEFICITS

The primary problem children with AS experience is difficulty in social interactions (Broderick *et al.* 2002). Although these children generally want to interact with others, they lack the social skills to do so effectively and smoothly (Koning and Magill-Evans 2001). These children are usually described as being socially odd or pedantic, and they are often thought of as being little professors (Attwood 2001). They do not fully know or understand the rules of social interaction that come naturally to most people (Krasny *et al.* 2003). For example, they often do not use appropriate eye contact, do not gesture appropriately, do not understand the give-and-take nature of social interactions, do not know how to initiate and maintain conversations, and do not respect the personal space of others (Attwood 2000; Koning and Magill-Evans 2001; Krasny *et al.* 2003). It is important to point out that these children generally are not acting out of defiance; instead, they simply do not understand the unspoken rules of social interaction. It is as if they are trying to play a game without knowing the rules, which is a recipe for disaster. Children usually pick up on the rules of social interaction naturally as they mature and do not have to be explicitly taught things, such as how far away to stand from someone when talking with them or to make eye contact when talking with someone. In contrast, individuals with AS require direct teaching of these social inter-action rules.

Children with AS often become socially isolated because they come across as being so socially awkward (Klin *et al.* 2000). When children with AS try to have a con-versation with someone, it generally ends up being one-sided and is not back and forth in nature (Attwood 2000; Koning and Magill-Evans 2001). In other words, they tend to monopolize the conversation with their own interests and do not appropriately engage the other person (Zwaigenbaum and Szatmari 1999). Even when they generally focus on their special topic(s) of interest and usually avoid topics that involve emotions or feelings. In fact, when others share emotions with them, these children generally do not respond appropriately or supportively. As a result, their seeming lack of concern or empathy often gets interpreted as rudeness, and this can certainly harm the quality of their friendships and other social relationships (Krasny *et al.* 2003).

Children with AS tend to ignore others' nonverbal behaviors and, therefore, often miss important social cues that may indicate the other person is bored or frustrated. When they do pay attention to nonverbal behaviors of others, they tend to misinterpret the cues, which again can lead to problems in their social relationships (Williams 1995). Children with AS also have great difficulty correctly interpreting tones of voice and facial expressions in other people (Lindner and Rosén in press). For example, they may not pick up on a sarcastic tone of voice and therefore may mistakenly believe that someone has just complimented them when the person has just insulted or teased them. Large misunderstandings like this can cause significant problems within social relationships. Children with AS often have relationships with others, but these rela-tionships tend to be strained or conflicted due to their problems with social skills (Attwood 2003).

RESTRICTED PATTERNS OF INTEREST

Many children with AS have a specific topic that is of great interest to them (APA 2000). These interests are not simply a hobby or pastime; instead, they typically spend large amounts of time talking about or participating in their area of special interest. Children with AS often compile enormous amounts of information about their special topic of interest and "share" this knowledge with others, regardless of the other person's level of interest in the topic (Williams 1995). Many times they fill their free time with collecting more facts and information about their special topic, often to the point of not playing like most children do (Zwaigenbaum and Szatmari 1999).

The topic of interest can be just about anything—it is the intensity of the interest that is diagnostic. Some examples of the wide range of special topics of interest are: trains, sprinklers, opera, computers/technology, vacuum cleaners, weather patterns, and so forth. It can be difficult to determine if the child has a special interest because the topic of interest may be popular among most peers. For example, some children with AS have special interests in computers, video games, or other popular games. In these instances, it is the intensity of the interest and the amount of knowledge about the topic that distinguishes children with AS from their typically developing peers. Children with AS will know far more about the topic than other children and will have collected countless facts about it.

LANGUAGE DEVELOPMENT

By definition, children with AS do not have a significant delay in their language development, such as when they said their first word or when they began talking in sentences (APA 2000). Although children with AS understand the semantics of language, they have problems in how they use language (Zwaigenbaum and Szatmari 1999). They may speak using an odd tone of voice, inflection, volume, or speed (Klin *et al.* 2000). For example, their tone of voice may not match what they are saying; they may be reporting that a family pet died, yet their tone of voice may not sound sad. In fact, they often come across as sounding "matter of fact" or as having a "flat" tone of voice, meaning that their voice inflection is neutral, regardless of what they are saying (Klin *et al.* 2000). Thus, while children with AS develop language normally, they have difficulty with the usage of language, especially in social situations.

PREVALENCE

The information available regarding the number of people with AS is limited. The *DSM-IV-TR* simply states that prevalence information is "lacking" (APA 2000). There are, however, some estimates available. Gillberg and Gillberg (1989) estimated that 3.6 children out of 1,000 have AS. When Ehlers and Gillberg (1993) included children who were "at risk" of having AS, they found a prevalence rate of 7.1 per 1,000 children. With regard to gender differences, more males than females are affected by AS, with ratios ranging from 4:1 to 2.3:1 (Ehlers and Gillberg 1993).

Assessment issues

Assessment for AS should always be done by a qualified professional with experience in autism spectrum disorders (ASDs). A very important part of an AS assessment is a complete developmental and health history. Parents and other caregivers should play a large role in helping the person doing the assessment learn about the child's early development (Klin *et al.* 2000). Questions that the parents should be asked include: when they first had concerns, the child's language and motor development, and any special interests that the child may have. Because social skills are the key deficit in children with AS, the child's social development should receive extra attention. Questions related to social issues may include: specific problems noticed; friendship skills; development of friendships; and typical play behaviors.

One parent or caregiver interview that is often used is the Autism Diagnostic Interview–Revised (ADI-R; Lord, Rutter, and Le Couteur 1994). The information from the ADI-R can be used to help determine an appropriate diagnosis. The ADI-R focuses on the early developmental history of the child and can provide much of the information needed to decide between a diagnosis of autism and AS. While the ADI-R is certainly useful, it is generally quite time consuming and usually takes about two hours to complete.

An AS assessment should also include measures of the child's cognitive and adaptive functioning (Klin *et al.* 2000). Given that most children and adolescents with AS have average or above average IQs, a standardized verbal intelligence test such as the Wechsler Intelligence Scales for Children Fourth Edition (WISC-IV; Wechsler 2003) can be used. If there is a concern about the child's language abilities (i.e., receptive and expressive language), a nonverbal IQ test such as the Universal Nonverbal Intelligence Test (UNIT; Bracken and McCallum 1998) can be used. While it is important to know the child's IQ, it is also very important to assess the child's adaptive skills within real world settings, such as at home and at school (Klin *et al.* 2000). It is in this portion of the assessment that the child's daily living and independence skills are examined. One of the most widely used measures of adaptive functioning is the Vineland Adaptive Behavior Scales (Sparrow, Ball, and Cicchetti 1984a). This assesses the child's skill level in a number of areas, including communication, daily living skills, socialization, and motor skills. It is important to assess both the child's IQ and the child's adaptive functioning in order to see if there are any large differences between them (Klin *et al.* 2000).

Given that the key symptom of AS is social skills deficits, special attention should be given to assessing the child's existing social skills within real-life social settings. This can be accomplished by observing the child in his or her naturally occurring social settings such as on the playground, during recess, or during mealtimes (Klin *et al.* 2000). The observer should particularly watch for social skills such as:

- the child's ability to engage in social interactions with other children
- the amount of eye contact used when talking with others
- the ability to initiate and sustain conversation
- the ability to understand humor, sarcasm or irony
- the awareness of the need to adjust voice tone and volume appropriately.

Another measure often used is the Autism Diagnostic Observation Schedule (ADOS), which helps professionals identify children, adolescents, and adults with an ASD (Lord *et al.* 2000). The ADOS uses a series of activities that are designed to "set up" the child to display (or not display) characteristics often seen in children with ASD, which can assist greatly with the diagnostic process.

Parent report measures have also been developed to aid professionals in assessing for AS, and they have been the focus of some recent research (Kiker and Rosén 2003). Parent report measures are convenient because they can act as a brief screening for practitioners, especially considering the lengthy time requirements of the ADI-R and the ADOS. Some examples of parent report measures include:

- Australian Scale for Asperger's Syndrome (ASAS; Garnett and Attwood 1995)

- Autistic Spectrum Screening Questionnaire (ASSQ; Ehlers, Gillberg, and Wing 1999)

- Asperger Syndrome Diagnostic Scale (ASDS; Myles, Bock, and Simpson 2001)

- Gilliam Asperger's Disorder Scale (GADS; Gilliam 2001).

A recent study assessed the ability of the ASAS, ASSQ, and the ASDS to correctly identify children with AS and found that the ASAS was best, followed by the ASSQ and ASDS respectively (Kiker and Rosén 2003).

In summary, a complete assessment for AS should include a detailed developmental history, measures of cognitive and adaptive functioning, and observations of the child in real-life social settings. Additionally, a structured observation such as the ADOS is often quite useful in assessing for AS. Furthermore, parent and teacher report measures are generally helpful and require little time to complete. As with all psychological assessments, it is important to gather information from a number of different sources in order to decide on an appropriate diagnosis and treatment. Therefore, an AS assessment should provide a complete picture of the child, including the child's strengths and areas for growth.

3. The Importance of Social Skills

Research has shown that social skills deficits are the greatest challenge for children with Asperger's Syndrome (AS) (Church, Alisanki and Amanullah 2000). Because these children have such difficulty with social skills, they tend to struggle with developing age-appropriate friendships. Furthermore, while many children with AS want to have friendships, their social awkwardness may cause them to become socially isolated and/or rejected (Marriage *et al.* 1995).

Research has been done on children who have been labeled "social isolates." This term refers to children who are rejected socially, who are not accepted by other children, and who are socially withdrawn (Gottman 1977b). The results of these studies suggest that this pattern of social rejection and withdrawal can continue throughout childhood and even into adulthood (Evers-Pasquale and Sherman 1975). These are children who, like children with AS, have great difficulty in social interactions. When these socially rejected children try to interact with others, the interactions often end up being negative experiences, which can cause even further social rejection (Gottman 1977b). Thus, the social consequences of having poor social skills are long-lasting—these children not only have significant social difficulties in childhood, but also into adulthood.

The impact of peer rejection or isolation can be quite severe (Ladd 1981). For example, peer rejection and low popularity have been associated with delinquent behavior, dropping out of school, and mental health issues (Gottman 1977a; Ladd 1981). Unpopular children are also more likely to be underachievers in school, to have learning difficulties, to have behavioral problems, and to have mental health problems as adults (Putallaz and Gottman 1981). In addition, it has been found that the level of peer acceptance during elementary school predicts later emotional adjustment and functioning (La Greca and Santogrossi 1980).

It is quite obvious that social skills deficits can have serious negative consequences. The effects of having poor social skills have also been examined by those who specifically study children with AS. It has been found that when children do not have good friendship skills, the negative effects are long-lasting and affect cognitive, social, and emotional development (Attwood 2003). The skills children learn during childhood by playing with other children act as stepping stones to the skills needed to be a successful adult. Children with AS often miss out on these learning opportunities due to their social skills deficits (Attwood 2003). Some examples of the skills learned during childhood play include: problem solving, conflict resolution, respecting the ideas of others, cooperation, and teamwork. These are skills that are often the basis of long-term relationships, both personal and business. In addition, individuals with AS generally have more negative social experiences, which places them at higher risk of developing low self-esteem and/or depression (Broderick *et al.* 2002).

It is clearly very important to help children with AS improve their social skills, given that they are at higher risk of experiencing the negative social consequences discussed above. Research suggests that improving the social skills of children on the autism spectrum is one of the most powerful predictors of a positive outcome (Kanner, Rodriguez, and Ashenden 1972; Mesibov 1984).

While it is well known that social skills are the largest challenge for children with AS, little is known about how to best teach these social skills (Attwood 2000; Mesibov 1984; Weiss and Harris 2001). Many professionals have treated these children, most commonly by teaching social skills in a group or individual setting, but no model treatment program has been specifically developed for leading these types of groups (Krasny *et al.* 2003). Although some social skills curricula for individuals with a high-functioning autism spectrum disorder have been developed, they are not specifically designed for a group format and do not outline the empirical basis of the skills and interventions used.

4. Treatment Approaches

Very few resources are available to clinicians and teachers who wish to lead social skills groups for children and adolescents with Asperger's Syndrome (AS). As a result, many are being forced to try and adapt social skills curricula for children with behavior disorders (Krasny *et al.* 2003). While some of the social skills deficits are similar in children with behavior disorders and children with autism spectrum disorders (ASDs), the underlying causes of their social difficulties are quite different.

Children with behavior disorders experience social skills deficits that stem from their problems with impulse control, emotion regulation, and compliance. In contrast, children with an ASD experience social skills deficits that stem from their lack of understanding of the rules of social interaction. Thus, children with ASDs need to be directly taught the specific rules of social interaction, while children with behavior disorders generally know these rules but fail to follow them.

Unfortunately, many of the programs designed for children with behavior disorders do not fully address the needs of children with ASDs (Krasny *et al.* 2003). The behavior disorder curriculum generally focuses more on problem resolution and emotion regulation skills than on issues more pertinent to children on the autism spectrum. Curricula for children with ASDs should highlight skills that are especially relevant to these children such as:

- reading and interpreting nonverbal communication (i.e., body language)
- maintaining appropriate eye contact
- learning personal space boundaries
- knowing when to talk about an area of special interest and when not to talk about the interest.

Social skills curricula designed for children with behavior disorders do address some basic social skills deficits but they generally do not take into account the very specific needs of children on the autism spectrum.

Summary of study findings

Previous studies have examined the potential effectiveness of social skills groups for children and adolescents on the autism spectrum (see Krasny *et al.* 2003). For a complete review of these studies, please refer to the Appendix: Theoretical Background to this Resource. A summary of the empirical findings will be presented here.

The studies that have examined social skills groups for children on the autism spectrum provide a starting point from which an empirically grounded program can be developed. The number of group members in these studies ranged from 5 to 15 and the groups met once weekly except for one study which met once monthly. The duration of the groups ranged widely, from 8 weeks to 4 years, although the majority were between 8 and 14 weeks in duration. There was variability in the length of each session; some groups were as short as 45 minutes, while others lasted up to two and a half hours. Some groups were potentially as long as four hours, in which one hour was spent on social skills instruction and the remaining two to three hours were spent in a recreational activity. Most groups, however, were between 45 minutes and 90 minutes in length.

The skills most often targeted in these groups included:

- meeting others

- emotion awareness and expression

- eye contact

- perspective-taking activities

- understanding and using nonverbal behavior

- conversational skills

- interpreting and using tone of voice

- giving and receiving compliments

- enjoying social interactions

- interviewing skills

- stress and anger management

- greetings

- interpreting a variety of social situations

- problem-solving skills

- teamwork

- appropriately sharing a topic of interest

- discovering the interests of others

- staying on track in conversations

- identifying and using appropriate facial expressions

- applying social skills in a recreational setting.

A variety of teaching techniques were used in the groups reviewed, but most included:

- modeling
- roleplaying
- coaching
- videotaped interactions
- structured games and activities
- positive reinforcement

- verbal feedback
- constructive feedback
- discussing real-life social experiences or situations
- visual supports
- community outings
- communication with parents.

Key components of a social skills group

Krasny and colleagues (2003) have identified ten "essential ingredients" to social skills programs for individuals with an ASD in response to the lack of a social skills curriculum for this population. First, it is important to make abstract concepts more concrete. The target behavior related to the social skill being taught should be clearly defined to the point that the children should be able to not only recognize it but should also be able to understand how it is different from other behaviors. A useful tool is to phrase social rules in an "if-then" fashion such as: if someone says "hello", then you say "hello". In addition, it is important to provide a number of behavior options for specific social situations, such as three things you can say when you are greeted by someone. Additionally, children on the autism spectrum generally learn best with visual supports in place. For example, if a child is not making eye contact with someone, a picture of eyes can be held up as a reminder cue. As group members master skills, the visual supports can be lessened.

Second, the group should be highly structured and predictable. One way to accomplish this goal is by having the basic format of the group remain the same regardless of the new skills and activities introduced each week. The group should follow a predictable sequence such as an opening, skill activities, and then a closing. A picture schedule could also be utilized to help transitions occur smoothly or to assist group members with an unexpected change in routine.

Third, transitions should be structured such that one activity naturally leads the group members into the next activity with minimal disruption. Group members can be given specific tasks that transition to the next activity, such as working in groups to put away materials and to get out the next set of materials. By virtue of this structure, the group members will be more focused on the task itself than on the more difficult transition.

Fourth, special attention should be paid to the varied cognitive and language abilities of children in the group, and these differences should be taken into consideration when planning the group. Children should be grouped by their language abilities because some children may require more visual supports than others and some may need very clear, concrete, and simple directions. Most children with AS, however, need fewer of these supports and are more independent with regard to using and understanding language.

Fifth, children on the autism spectrum have different learning styles and therefore, various teaching strategies should be used. For example, the target social skill can be presented in a number of different ways, using activities such as games, roleplays, reading tasks, writing tasks, gross motor tasks, art activities, and so on. By providing varied learning opportunities for the social skills being taught, the likelihood of effective learning increases.

Sixth, activities should be done in pairs or groups as much as possible in order to foster showing interest in others. The activities that are done in groups or pairs require group members to interact with one another, discover information about each other, and cooperate, which facilitates developing interest in others. For example, at the first group meeting, members can introduce others in the group instead of simply introducing themselves, and during snack time members can serve each other instead of just themselves.

Seventh, the group should address the tendency of children on the autism spectrum to have low self-esteem as a result of their social difficulties. Therefore, treatment should include concepts such as self-awareness, self-acceptance, and self-appreciation. Although the group members presumably have notable problems with social skills, the strengths of each member should be acknowledged whenever possible. Group members should be encouraged or required to compliment each other on a regular basis and some groups have done this at the end of each session as part of the closing routine. Activities that serve to help group members see what they have in common with other members are also helpful in promoting self-awareness and self-esteem.

Eighth, the goals of the group should be relevant specifically to children with an ASD and the activities used should be social in nature and/or focus on a social issue. Social skills that are key components of social interaction, such as eye contact, should be the main focus of the group as opposed to less central skills, such as negotiation. In addition, group members will likely learn more effectively when they have an understanding of the importance of the skill and recognize its applicability.

Ninth, the skills being taught should build upon each other—basic skills should be taught first and then more complex skills should be introduced. Basic skills are part of the more complex skills and these basic skills should continue to be reinforced throughout the group. Complex skills should be broken down into their component parts, taught in a sequential manner, and then integrated to demonstrate the complex skill. Skills learned early on in the group should continue to be highlighted in later group sessions.

Tenth, the issue of generalization of skills should be addressed. One potential problem with teaching children on the autism spectrum new skills is that while they may be able to demonstrate the skill in one setting, such as in group, they may not display that same skill in other settings, such as at home or school. As a result, the social skills taught in group should be practiced in a variety of community settings and with a variety of people. To promote generalization to the home environment, a parent handout can be given to parents each week which describes the target skill of that week and what parents can do at home to reinforce the skill. In addition, the group itself can be offered in a natural setting such as at school, but problems with generalization will likely remain because the group itself will probably not be held in each child's particular classroom. As an alternative, a handout similar to the parent handout can be given to the group members' classroom teachers to let the teachers know what skill was taught and what they can do to reinforce the skill. Lastly, outings into the community, such as to a restaurant or library, can provide group members with opportunities to practice their social skills in naturally occurring settings, and this may serve to increase the generalizability of the social skills they have learned.

5. Introduction to the Model Program

This model program is guided by the ten "essential ingredients" outlined by Krasny *et al.* (2003) and by the research studies reviewed (see Appendix). The model program is based on what was common procedure in the majority of the reviewed studies, and the logistics of the model program are based on the group therapy literature for children and adolescents as a whole.

There is no empirical support for an ideal length, frequency, or duration of a group. The literature, however, provides some guidance. One study that examined the effectiveness of groups for children and adolescents found that the length of group sessions had some impact on the effectiveness of the group intervention (Hoag 1996). It was determined that groups that were 60 minutes in length produced more positive results than those that met for a shorter time, but no further gains were made by the group being longer than 60 minutes. It was also found that the effectiveness of the group did not increase by meeting more than once per week. Additionally, it was found that there was no relationship between the number of sessions and the effectiveness of the group. Another study of groups for children with internalizing disorders found that the average number of sessions was seven, that the average length of the group was one hour, and that most groups met weekly (Grossman and Hughes 1992). A number of other studies have used a similar approach. For example, a group designed to teach social skills to children, although not children on the autism spectrum, met once per week for one hour and fifteen minutes (Swager 1995).

The studies specific to children and adolescents on the autism spectrum ranged in length from 45 minutes to two and a half hours, and most were between 45 and 90 minutes in length. These studies also ranged in duration from 8 weeks to 4 years, although most were between 8 and 14 weeks.

Based on the guidance of the literature, the following model program is designed to include ten, 60-minute group sessions on a weekly basis. A total of 23 sessions are included, however, such that the program can be adapted as needed.

The issue of number of participants seems to be most related to the number of staff available to lead the groups. All of the reviewed studies utilized roleplays, which requires a fairly small staff-participant ratio. It is recommended that the number of group members be limited based on the availability of staff. As a general rule, there should be one staff member per two to three children, in order to allow adult facilitation of roleplay pairs.

The majority of the studies reviewed included a less structured social time during group, usually a snack time. Therefore, a social snack time is included in the model program. It is important to note that while this time is less structured than other portions of the group, it is essential that staff facilitate this time. Staff should encourage group participants to interact with one another and provide feedback regarding their interactions. For example, staff can assist a group member in selecting an appropriate topic of discussion, prompt group members to ask a question if they have been talking for a while, and provide reminders of the basic rules of social interaction (e.g., look at the person talking). While raising hands to answer questions is quite appropriate during instructional times of group, participants should be encouraged to interact without raising their hands during social snack time. This will more closely simulate naturally occurring social situations and will also provide group members with the opportunity to determine when they should speak and when they should listen.

A number of the reviewed studies also included homework assignments and communication with parents and/or teachers. Toward this end, the model program includes parent and teacher handouts that can be distributed following the group session. In order to facilitate generalization of skills, it is important that parents and teachers be aware of the skills that are being taught in group so that they can encourage practice of the skills and provide appropriate feedback. The issue of confidentiality of treatment arises with the inclusion of teacher handouts and should be addressed as outlined by the particular setting in which the group will occur. For example, in a clinic setting, a release of information signed by the parent may be appropriate or group leaders may choose to give both handouts to the parent and allow the parent to directly share the handout with the teacher.

Each group session should be structured and follow a predictable routine. The model program is designed for participants to enter and greet each other informally with staff facilitation while waiting for all group members to arrive. The next portion of the group is direct instruction and related activities. The following portion of group is the social snack time. The final portion of the group is the closing in which members should appropriately tell one another goodbye and the parent and teacher handouts are distributed.

The skills presented in the model program are introduced such that they build upon previously presented skills. Research argues for teaching social skills in a sequential and progressive manner, and the model program is designed keeping this concept in mind. Throughout the entire progression of the group sessions, basic, foundational skills (e.g., eye contact) should be consistently practiced and reinforced.

It is also recommended that visual supports be utilized when teaching the component skills of more complex social skills. For example, a card with a picture of eyes on it and the words "eyes on me" or "make eye contact" are useful tools, and can act as noninvasive visual reminders for group participants. Other cards could include relevant pictures and words such as: "ask me a question now," "ask me how I am feeling," "stop talking," and "your turn to talk."

6. Summing Up

This resource has been designed to assist clinicians and teachers with leading social skills groups for children and adolescents with Asperger's Syndrome (AS). It is an empirically grounded model program that specifically addresses the social skills deficits often found in children and adolescents with AS. The empirical basis for each skill has been provided and the relevant literature has been used to guide the creation of this model program. Although the literature regarding the effectiveness of social skills groups for individuals with AS is growing, further research is still needed. In the meantime, children and adolescents with AS need appropriate treatment and intervention, as they simply cannot wait for the help they require. It is hoped that this empirically grounded resource will help provide that much-needed intervention.

The ten core sessions are considered the essential, most fundamental, and basic social skills that are needed to foster successful social interactions. These core social skills are well discussed in the literature and have been frequently addressed in studies examining the efficacy of social skills groups for children and adolescents with an autism spectrum disorder (ASD). The supplemental sessions have been included to buttress the ten core sessions, providing more activities for the skills and introducing additional social skills. The supplemental sessions are intended to allow professionals to customize their social skills groups to meet the needs of the group members. The supplemental sessions are also empirically grounded and the empirical basis for each of the skills is provided.

While this model program is designed to be "ready-to-use," it is always important to take into consideration the particular needs of the individuals. In addition, it is well documented in the literature that children with social skills deficits are at greater risk to develop other mental health issues (La Greca and Santogrossi 1980; Ladd 1981; Putallaz and Gottman 1981). Given this knowledge, it is important to monitor group members for potential "comorbid" (concurrent) mental health issues. When comorbid mental health issues are present, it is best to treat those issues in a separate treatment setting. This is important because the group focus is on general difficulties associated with having an ASD and cannot adequately address a specific child's comorbid mental health needs (Howlin and Yates 1999).

While parent handouts are included in the model program, these handouts are not intended to replace ongoing communication with the parents of the group members. In fact, active involvement of parents has been identified as a key component to a successful social skills program (Bloomquist 1996; O'Callaghan *et al.* 2003). More specifically, it is important that group leaders consistently communicate with the parent regarding issues such as the child's level of participation, behavioral concerns, individual strengths and weaknesses, any concerns about comorbid mental health issues, and so forth. If there are concerns about comorbid mental health issues, group leaders should communicate these concerns to the parent and make appropriate treatment recommendations, such as individual and/or family therapy.

This model program has been designed to utilize a number of teaching approaches, the most obvious being direct instruction to the group members. In addition, parent and teacher handouts have been included to communicate the specific skills that were covered in group and to provide suggestions regarding how the skills learned in group can be reinforced at home and at school. It is hoped that the various empirically grounded teaching approaches used in this model program will assist children and adolescents with AS in acquiring the social skills needed to foster successful social interactions.

PART II

THE PROGRAM

7. The Model Program

Group session topics

Session 1: Greetings and getting to know you

Session 2: Identifying emotions

Session 3: Identifying facial expressions

Session 4: Continuum of emotions

Session 5: Tone of voice

Session 6: Initiating conversations

Session 7: Maintaining conversations: Basic conversational skills

Session 8: Maintaining conversations: Responding to the emotions of others

Session 9: Conversational skills: Phone skills

Session 10: Manners and dinner outing

These topics were chosen because they are the basic, foundational skills needed to have more successful social interactions with others. In addition, these areas are ones that are well addressed in the research literature. In fact, each session outlines the empirical basis for that session's particular skill. The sequence of the session topics was designed to start with foundational skills and then move to more complex skills. Furthermore, the sequence was chosen to allow the group members to first learn the basic skills that they will need in order to be able to successfully learn subsequent skills. For example, in order to engage in a conversation, group members must be able to appropriately greet others, identify basic emotions in others both through body language and tone of voice, and have the skills to initiate a conversation. The topic of phone skills is considered a more complex skill than typical conversational skills, because phone skills require sole reliance on the other person's tone of voice (nonverbal cues such as facial expression are not present). Finally, a community outing is the most complex because it requires the implementation and integration of all the learned skills.

Session 1: Greetings and getting to know you

Aim of session

The aim of this group session is to acquaint the group members with one another, practice meeting new people, and learn the basic component skills to greetings.

Empirical basis for the skill

Greetings and introductions are well addressed in the literature (Mesibov 1984; Provencal 2003). Many studies also address this issue, covering topics such as initiating conversations and entering a group already engaged in an activity, both of which require the use of greetings and introductions (Cragar and Horvath 2003; Heitzman-Powell 2003; Howlin and Yates 1999; Ozonoff and Miller 1995). Greetings and introductions are usually the first portion of an interaction and generally contribute heavily to the "first impression" of someone.

Introduce greetings

First, review with the group members the importance of making good first impressions, highlighting that this is one of the first steps in making friends. Discuss with the group the ways in which people greet one another. Group leaders should also help group members brainstorm how they might greet others differently depending upon the situation and who the other person is. For example, one would use a more formal greeting to meet an adult such as a principal, leader of an organization (i.e., Boy Scouts, Girl Scouts, etc.), or a teacher. A less formal greeting would be used when meeting another child in an informal setting, such as at recess, in the lunchroom, or at a party. A more formal greeting would include standing, holding out your hand to handshake, saying "Hello, I am _____," and then stating something such as "It's nice to meet you." A less formal greeting would include staying in your seated or standing position, and saying "Hi, I'm _____." The component skills of greetings include: making eye contact, determining appropriate physical distance, and smiling at the other person.

Greetings activity

Now have the group members practice introducing themselves to each other both formally and informally. One way to make this activity more enjoyable and to assure that all group members will fully participate is to have them write their names on labels. Each group member should write their name on as many labels as there are group members, minus one. Then they should introduce themselves to the other group members and at each interaction, group members should exchange name stickers. At the end of the activity, each group member should have stickers with the names of all other members and none of their own stickers. Group leaders should facilitate this activity and provide group members with feedback about their use of greetings.

Introduce getting to know others

Next, group leaders should discuss with the group how to get to know others that they have not met previously. Facilitate a discussion of appropriate conversation topics and questions when meeting someone new. Examples would include asking about and sharing: school of attendance, interests, basic family information (i.e., brothers, sisters), neighborhood of residence, and so forth.

Getting to know others activity

Introduce the "Everyone Who" game to the group (see below). Group leaders are encouraged to participate so that they can facilitate the group members' interactions and so that the group members can learn about the group leaders as well.

"Everyone Who" Game

Materials

- Chairs

Directions

Group members are seated in their chairs in a circle formation. One group member should be standing in the middle of the circle and his or her chair should be removed from the circle, giving one less chair than total number of group participants. The person in the middle completes the statement "everyone who _____." Examples include, "everyone who":

- likes pizza
- has a sister/brother
- likes to play video games
- wishes it were summertime
- is wearing sneakers.

Those in the group who agree with the statement made must get up and find a new chair to sit in, and the person in the middle also tries to find a chair to sit in. Therefore, at the end of each round, a person will be left standing, and this person gets to make the next statement.

The "Everyone Who" game is designed to facilitate the group members learning about others in the group, and group leaders should highlight for the participants the commonalities that are discovered through the game by pointing out their observations and asking questions of the participants. For example, if two group members like to play a particular video game, group leaders should point out this common interest and suggest potential conversation topics (i.e., what level each of them have made it to, what their favorite parts of the game are, and so forth).

Snack and social time

During snack time, group members should be encouraged to use the information they learned about one another in their social conversations. It is essential that group leaders facilitate social interactions during snack time. During this session in particular, group leaders should focus on helping group members discuss common interests and basic personal information.

Closing

At the end of the session, group members should be encouraged to appropriately tell each other goodbye and that they will see each other again next week. If there are any special upcoming occasions (e.g., birthdays, vacations, holidays), they should be encouraged to acknowledge them to one another. Distribute parent handouts to the parents and also provide parents with a copy of the teacher handout that they can share with their children's teachers.

Session 1: Greetings and getting to know you

PARENT HANDOUT

What we did during group today

Today we worked on how to introduce ourselves to others both formally and informally. We discussed in which situations formal and informal greetings should be used. We practiced introducing ourselves to other members in the group. We also played a game in which we were able to get to know each other and discover similarities among ourselves. We then used these similarities as the starting point for conversations during social snack time.

What to work on at home

You can practice introductions and greetings with your child at home by roleplaying. You can also encourage him or her to identify situations in which a formal or informal introduction would be most appropriate. Quiz your child about this throughout the week as you encounter various social situations. As you and your child encounter situations appropriate for introductions, encourage him or her to first determine which type of introduction to use, and to then introduce himself or herself to others. This is a great way for your child to get to know others and to broaden his or her social circles.

Session 1: Greetings and getting to know you

TEACHER HANDOUT

What we did in group this week

This week we worked on how to introduce ourselves to others both formally and informally. We discussed in which situations formal and informal greetings should be used. We practiced introducing ourselves to other members in the group. We also played a game in which we were able to get to know each other and discover similarities among ourselves. We then used these similarities as the starting point for conversations during social snack time.

What to work on at school

At school, you can help the child to determine which situations call for informal and formal greetings, such as at recess, at lunch, and when meeting the principal or a new teacher. You can roleplay with the child various social situations that call for greetings in the school setting. You can also facilitate the child introducing him or herself to other children and school staff. This is a great way for the child to get to know others and to broaden his or her social circles.

Session 2: Identifying emotions

Aim of session

The aim of this group session is to assist the group members in being able to both identify and express basic emotions.

Empirical basis for the skill

Emotional awareness, including identifying and expressing emotions, is well addressed in the literature (Marriage *et al.* 1995; Mesibov 1985; Provencal 2003; Williams 1989). More specifically, identifying facial expressions is a component skill of correctly identifying emotions in others. Barnhill and colleagues (2002) explicitly address identifying facial expressions.

Introduce emotions

Group leaders should facilitate a discussion of the wide variety of emotions people feel. Examples include:

- happy
- sad
- scared
- excited
- surprised
- embarrassed
- tired
- bored.

Group leaders should ask group members to briefly share situations that make them feel these various emotions.

Introduce identifying emotions

Group leaders should ask group members how they know what others are feeling, and should highlight the importance of recognizing facial expressions. Group members can then briefly practice their facial expressions and have other group members guess the emotion. For example, they can display for one another their "happy faces," "sad faces," "excited faces," "scared faces," and so on. Group leaders should facilitate group members in pointing out specific features of the person making the facial expression that led them to guess the correct emotion, helping group members point out specific characteristics of the facial expression that are key components. For example, for a surprised facial expression, facial cues would include the eyebrows being raised, the eyes being widely opened, and the mouth being opened somewhat.

Introduce "Feeling Charades" game

Introduce the game "Feeling Charades" to the group (see below). Group leaders should facilitate the game, providing appropriate feedback to the group members and highlighting key components to accurately identify facial expressions.

"Feeling Charades" Game

Materials

- Emotion cards
- Container

Emotion cards are cards or slips of paper that have an emotion word listed on them. These should be emotions that were covered in the earlier group discussion of emotions and identifying facial expressions. It is also helpful to group members if both the emotion word and a sketch of the facial expression are on the card.

Directions

The emotion cards should be prepared prior to the group and should be placed in a container. One group member should be selected to start the game, perhaps a member who has displayed exceptional behavior such as following directions or participating well in group. This group member should first choose an emotion card out of the container and not reveal to other group members the emotion he or she drew from the container. He or she should then stand in front of the group and display the facial expression that corresponds to the emotion drawn from the container. The other group members should then guess the emotion. Once the correct emotion has been guessed, group leaders should assist the group members in identifying the characteristics of the facial expression that led them to correctly guess the emotion. Then, another group member should choose an emotion card from the container. A method of determining which group member goes next should be chosen that ensures that every group member has the chance to draw an emotion from the container.

Snack and social time

Group members should be encouraged to identify how others in the group are feeling based on their facial expressions during their conversations with one another. Again, it is essential that group leaders facilitate social interactions during snack time. During this snack time, each child should have their photograph taken expressing at least three emotions: happy, sad, and mad. These photographs will be used for next week's group.

It will be important for the person taking the photographs to write an "answer key" to the facial expression pictures being taken, as some group members' facial expressions may be difficult to recognize.

Closing

At the end of the session, group members should be encouraged to appropriately tell each other goodbye and that they will see each other again next week. If there are any special upcoming occasions (e.g., birthdays, vacations, holidays), group members should be encouraged to acknowledge them to one another. Distribute parent handouts to the parents and also provide parents with a copy of the teacher handout that they can share with their children's teachers.

Session 2: Identifying emotions

PARENT HANDOUT

What we did during group today

Today we worked on identifying emotions. We discussed different situations that cause us to feel various emotions. We then talked about how we can tell what others are feeling based on their facial expressions. Next, we practiced identifying emotions by playing the "Feeling Charades" game. In this game, we guessed the emotions of others who were making a facial expression. We talked about how we knew which emotion to guess based on characteristics of their faces (e.g., smiling).

What to work on at home

You can practice identifying emotions with your child by asking him or her to guess what you or other family members are feeling based on facial expressions. In fact, you can play "Feeling Charades" with your child at home. In addition, when you are out and about with your child, you can ask him or her at appropriate times to guess how others are feeling. One great way to do this is by "people watching" through a window while eating lunch, dinner, or a snack and asking your child to guess how others are feeling by looking at their facial expressions. You can also point out to your child how you think he or she is feeling based on your child's facial expression, which will also foster your child's awareness of his or her own emotions. For example, you could say things such as, "I can tell you are feeling happy right now because you are smiling."

Session 2: Identifying emotions

TEACHER HANDOUT

What we did in group this week

This week we worked on identifying emotions. We discussed different situations that cause us to feel various emotions. We then talked about how we can tell what others are feeling based on their facial expressions. Next, we practiced identifying emotions by playing the "Feeling Charades" game. In this game, we guessed the emotions of others who were making a facial expression. We talked about how we knew which emotion to guess based on characteristics of their faces (e.g., smiling).

What to work on at school

At school, you can help the child determine others' emotions by keying into facial expressions. You can ask the child to guess your emotion based upon your facial expression. You can also ask the child to determine the emotions of other students at school. For example, you and the child could stand on the edge of the field during recess for a few brief minutes and have him or her discreetly guess the emotions of a few other students. In addition, you can help the child become more aware of his or her own emotions by pointing out to the child how you think he or she is feeling based on facial expression. For example, you could say things such as, "I can tell you are feeling happy right now because you are smiling."

Session 3: Identifying facial expressions

Aim of session
The aim of this group session is to assist the group members in being able to identify their own and others' facial expressions accurately.

Empirical basis for the skill
Identification of facial expressions is addressed in the literature (Barnhill *et al.* 2002). More broadly, identifying and expressing emotions is a recurring theme in the literature (Marriage *et al.* 1995; Mesibov 1985; Provencal 2003; Williams 1989). Being able to accurately identify facial expressions serves to increase emotional awareness.

Introduce "Name that Emotion" game
Group leaders should remind the group members of the pictures that were taken at the end of last week's group and let them know that they will be asked to identify the emotions of both themselves and other group members. Group leaders should explain the "Name that Emotion" game to the group members (see below).

"Name that Emotion" Game

Materials
- Pictures of group members displaying at least three different emotions (i.e., happy, sad, and mad)
- Answer key to the facial expression pictures
- Paper and pencils for the group members to write their answers on
- Mirror

Directions
First, divide the group members into two teams and distribute a piece of paper and a pencil to each team. Explain that they will be shown the pictures taken from last week and will be asked to identify the emotion of the person in the picture as a team. Remind the group members of the choices: happy, sad, or mad. Explain that they are to write down their team answer for each picture shown. One group leader should be on each team to assist with conflict management and to remind the teams to be quiet in their discussions, so as to not let the other team know their answer. The group leaders should also help facilitate discussion among the group members while they try to determine the emotion of the person in the picture, encouraging them to verbalize what about the face led them to their answer.

Once all of the pictures have been shown and the teams have completed the answer sheets, the group should review the correct answers. Likely, group members will be surprised by some of the correct answers. When this occurs, the mirror should be given to the group member whose photo was difficult to identify. Group leaders should then facilitate group members giving this individual feedback about how to improve his or her facial expression for that emotion. The individual should use the mirror to help him or her see what should be changed to improve the facial expression. Group leaders should encourage group members to provide positive feedback to the individual when he or she has appropriately "fixed" the facial expression.

Snack and social time

Group members should again be encouraged to identify how others in the group are feeling based on their facial expressions during their conversations with one another. They should also be encouraged to engage in chit-chat with one another, as they have gotten to know more about one another over the past few weeks. Again, it is essential that group leaders facilitate social interactions during snack time.

Closing

At the end of the session, group members should be encouraged to appropriately tell each other goodbye and that they will see each other again next week. If there are any special upcoming occasions (e.g., birthdays, vacations, holidays), group members should be encouraged to acknowledge them to one another. Distribute parent handouts to the parents and also provide parents with a copy of the teacher handout that they can share with their children's teachers.

✓

Session 3: Identifying facial expressions

PARENT HANDOUT

What we did during group today

Today we continued to work on identifying emotions, especially with regard to correctly identifying emotions through facial expressions. We discussed the importance of being able to correctly identify the emotions of others by looking at their facial expressions—accurately identifying the emotions of others helps us know how to approach and/or talk to others. We played "Name that Emotion" game in which we identified the emotions of ourselves and other group members in photographs. We helped each other "perfect" our happy, sad, and mad faces by using mirrors to look at our own facial expressions.

What to work on at home

You can continue to practice identifying emotions with your child by asking him or her to guess how you or other family members are feeling based on facial expressions. Another great way to help your child become more aware of facial expressions is to stand with your child in front of a mirror and practice making various facial expressions with him or her. Help your child "perfect" his or her facial expressions and encourage your child to give you feedback on your facial expressions (i.e., you might make facial expressions that are not completely accurate).

Session 3: Identifying facial expressions

TEACHER HANDOUT

What we did in group this week

This week we continued to work on identifying emotions, especially with regard to correctly identifying emotions through facial expressions. We discussed the importance of being able to correctly identify the emotions of others by looking at their facial expressions—accurately identifying the emotions of others helps us know how to approach and/or talk to others. We played the "Name that Emotion" game in which we identified the emotions of ourselves and other group members in photographs. We helped each other "perfect" our happy, sad, and mad faces by using mirrors to look at our own facial expressions.

What to work on at school

At school, you can continue to help the child determine others' emotions by asking the child to guess your emotion based upon your facial expression. You can make "inaccurate" facial expressions and ask the child to help you "fix" your facial expression. When the child is making a facial expression, you can tell the child which emotion you think he or she is displaying. If you have a mirror handy in your classroom, you can hand the mirror to the child and point out the characteristics of his or her facial expression that you noticed and which led you to choose that particular emotion.

Session 4: Continuum of emotions

Aim of session

The aim of this group session is to help group members understand that there is a continuum of emotions. Now that they have an understanding of some basic emotions, the goal of this group session is to highlight that there are different degrees of various emotions.

Empirical basis for the skill

Emotional awareness is well addressed in the literature (Marriage *et al.* 1995; Mesibov 1985; Provencal 2003; Williams 1989). Part of emotional awareness is understanding the subtle differences within the same emotion, such as content, happy, and elated. Again, understanding this more subtle difference in emotions is helpful in interacting socially with others.

Introduce continuum of emotions

Group leaders should first praise the group members for their hard work in the past few weeks as they have worked on accurately identifying emotions. They should then facilitate a discussion of how people can feel different "degrees" of an emotion. For example, the group could discuss that the emotion "happy" has different degrees: content, happy, and elated. Group leaders should assist the group in discussing the degrees of a few different emotions such as happy, scared, mad, and sad.

Group leaders should then ask group members to briefly think of different situations that would cause them to feel these different degrees of an emotion and explain them to the group. For example, a child may feel content if he or she finds a sticker or small toy, happy if he or she has no homework for the evening, and elated if his or her parents said the family is going on a trip to Disney World.

Introduce "Continuum of Emotions" game

Group leaders should introduce the "Continuum of Emotions" game to the group (see below). Depending upon the size of the group, they may need to divide the group members into two groups for this activity and lead them separately.

"Continuum of Emotions" Game

Materials

- Tape
- Pieces of paper
- Marker

Directions

Group leaders should lay a piece of tape across the length of the floor, which will represent the continuum of emotions. They should then decide upon an emotion and ask the group to determine three "degrees" of that emotion. Listed below are some examples that can be used in this game:

- happy: content, happy, elated/overjoyed
- sad: upset, sad, depressed/devastated
- mad: annoyed, mad, furious
- scared: apprehensive/nervous, scared, terrified.

When the group has determined the three degrees of one emotion, the words chosen should be written on a piece of paper and placed at the ends and the middle of the piece of tape in order, representing a continuum of that emotion. Then group leaders should pose a situation to the group and ask them to stand where they think they would feel, given the situation. Group members will likely stand at different points along the continuum and group leaders should ask a few group members to briefly explain why they chose their spot on the continuum. Repeat the same procedure for each emotion covered. Group leaders can pose a few different situations per emotion before moving on to the next emotion.

Continuum of emotions scenario ideas

The following are ideas for scenarios to present to the group. Group leaders are encouraged to individualize the scenarios.

1. Another student called you a name.
2. The person sitting behind you in class keeps banging his or her pencil on the desk.
3. You got an "A" on your science test.
4. Your family is going on vacation to a place you've always wanted to go.
5. You are studying hard for a test tomorrow.
6. You lost your favorite video game.
7. Your parent just told you that a family pet died.
8. You found some change (money) on the sidewalk.
9. You accidentally left your homework at home and now you can not turn it in. You have to tell your teacher and you may get a zero for the assignment.
10. You are about to go through a "haunted house" on Halloween.

The "Continuum of Emotions" game is designed not only to help group members gain an understanding of the different "degrees" of emotions, but also to help them see that given the same situation, people can react with different degrees of the same emotion.

Snack and social time

During snack time, group members should be encouraged to chat with one another about their lives, including for example issues related to school and family. They could also discuss events in their lives such as vacations and ask the person telling the story how they felt during that time, as well as other appro- priate questions. Group leaders can highlight the various degrees of emotion that arise. Again, it is essential that they facilitate social interactions during snack time.

Closing

At the end of the session, group members should be encouraged to appropriately tell each other goodbye and that they will see each other again next week. If there are any special upcoming occasions (e.g., birthdays, vacations, holidays), group members should be encouraged to acknowledge them to one another. Distribute parent handouts to the parents and also provide parents with a copy of the teacher handout that they can share with their children's teachers.

Session 4: Continuum of emotions

PARENT HANDOUT

What we did during group today

Today we talked about how people can feel the same basic emotion but can feel different "degrees" of that emotion. For example, we talked about how people can feel content, happy, or elated. We played the "Continuum of Emotions" game. In this game we decided on the different degrees of an emotion and put them on a long piece of tape, representing the continuum of emotion. Next, we were presented with different situations and then we picked a spot to stand on the tape representing how we would feel, given that situation. We learned that there are different degrees to emotions and that different people can feel different degrees of emotion, even given the same situation.

What to work on at home

You can talk with your child about how people, including family members, can feel different degrees of the same emotion. You can use specific emotion language with your child to highlight this. For example, instead of saying that you feel scared, you could say you feel nervous or apprehensive. In addition, when your child expresses a feeling, ask your child what "degree" of that emotion he or she is feeling.

✓

Session 4: Continuum of emotions

TEACHER HANDOUT

What we did in group this week

This week we talked about how people can feel the same basic emotion but can feel different "degrees" of that emotion. For example, we talked about how people can feel content, happy, or elated. We played the "Continuum of Emotions" game. In this game we decided on the different degrees of an emotion and put them on a long piece of tape, representing the continuum of emotion. Next, we were presented with different situations and then we picked a spot to stand on the tape representing how we would feel, given that situation. We learned that there are different degrees to emotions and that different people can feel different degrees of emotion, even given the same situation.

What to work on at school

At school, you can talk with the child about how people, including teachers and classmates, can feel different degrees of the same emotion. You can use specific emotion language with the child to highlight this. For example, instead of saying that you feel scared, you could say you feel nervous or apprehensive. In addition, when the child expresses a feeling, ask the child what "degree" of that emotion he or she is feeling.

Session 5: Tone of voice

Aim of session

The aim of this group session is to help group members recognize that tone of voice plays a large role in understanding the meaning and emotion of statements.

Empirical basis for the skill

Nonverbal communication is discussed in the literature (Howlin and Yates 1999; Marriage *et al.* 1995; Ozonoff and Miller 1995; Williams 1989). Barnhill and colleagues (2002) specifically discuss the role that tone of voice plays in understanding meaning and determining emotion. In addition, Lindner and Rosén (in press) found that children with AS have great difficulty accurately identifying the emotions of others based solely on the tone of voice used. As such, a supplemental session has been included to further address identifying emotions solely through tone of voice (see Supplemental Session 2).

Introduce tone of voice

Group leaders should introduce the topic of tone of voice and the role it plays in understanding meaning and determining the emotion of the person speaking. They should then facilitate a discussion of how changing your tone of voice changes the emotion of the statement, regardless of the content of the statement. They should ask group members to give examples of their "sad" tones of voice, their "happy" tones of voice, their "mad" tones of voice, and so on. Be sure to cover the following tones of voice, as they will be used in the group activity:

- happy
- sad
- mad
- neutral.

Then, group leaders should challenge the group members to make one statement but state it with two different tones of voice. They should highlight for the group members that in today's group session, the focus will be on tone of voice, not the content of the statement. Thus, although the content of the statement might be sad (i.e., "My pet turtle died"), the focus is on the tone of voice the person used.

Introduce "Tone of Voice Jeopardy" game

Group leaders should introduce the game, "Tone of Voice Jeopardy" (see below), and should again point out that the game focuses on tone of voice, not the content of the statement.

"Tone of Voice Jeopardy" game

Materials

- Statement cards with determined tone of voice
- Piece of paper or a chalkboard to keep score
- Bells or other noisemaking device for participants to "ring in" to give their answer
- Small prize

Directions

Prior to the start of group, group leaders should make the statement cards. These cards consist of any brief statement, such as "I went to the store today," "dogs are nice," or "blue is my favorite color." On the cards, group leaders should write in which tone of voice the statement should be made. For simplicity, it is generally a good idea to narrow the choices down to: happy, sad, mad, or neutral tone of voice.

Explain to the group members that they will be asked to listen to a statement and then decide which tone of voice was used to state it. Let the group members know that their choices are: happy, sad, mad, or neutral tone of voice. Depending on the size of the group, group leaders may choose to divide group members into pairs or teams. For smaller groups, each group member can participate as an individual. A bell or other noisemaking device should be placed in front of each group member or team. Given that group members tend to get very excited while playing this game, group leaders should explicitly state that participants are to ring the bell only once. It is helpful if each team or participant has a different noisemaking device, as then it is easier to determine who "rang in" first.

Once everything is set up and group members have been introduced to the game, a group leader reads a statement in the predetermined tone of voice twice. After the group leader has finished reading, participants may "ring in" with their answer. Whoever rings in first with the correct answer receives one point. The team or person who provides the correct answer should explain to the group how they determined the correct tone of voice. The team or individual with the most points at the end of the game wins the small prize.

One potential problem that may arise when playing "Tone of Voice Jeopardy" is that group members may become upset if they or their team are not winning. As such, it is important that group leaders facilitate the game. To encourage group members to be good sports, group leaders can hand out small stickers, sweets, or other little prizes to group members who are being good sports. In fact, being a good sport is a skill that can help individuals with AS have more positive experiences with peers, especially at recess or other times when competitive games are generally played. This is the topic of a supplemental group session (see Supplemental Session 4).

Snack and social time

During snack time, group members should be encouraged to talk with other group members, paying close attention to their own tone of voice and the tone of voice of others. Group leaders should help facilitate this and point out the use of tone of voice when they notice group members using a particular tone of voice.

Closing

At the end of the session, group members should be encouraged to appropriately tell each other goodbye and that they will see each other again next week. If there are any special upcoming occasions (e.g., birthdays, vacations, holidays), group members should be encouraged to acknowledge them to one another. Distribute parent handouts to the parents and also provide parents with a copy of the teacher handout that they can share with their children's teachers.

Session 5: Tone of voice

PARENT HANDOUT

What we did during group today

Today we talked about how important tone of voice can be in understanding the meaning of a statement and in determining the emotion of the person talking. We also played "Tone of Voice Jeopardy." In this game we guessed the tone of voice being used—happy, sad, mad, or neutral. We learned that tone of voice is different than the content of a statement. In fact, we practiced saying the same statement using different tones of voice.

What to work on at home

You can talk with your child about the importance of paying attention to others' tones of voice to determine meaning and emotion and the importance of using tone of voice to communicate emotion to others. You can practice making statements using different tones of voice and having your child guess the tone of voice you used. You can also point out to your child that you can tell how he or she is feeling based on the tone of voice used. For example you could say, "I can tell you are feeling upset because you are using a mad tone of voice."

Session 5: Tone of voice

TEACHER HANDOUT

What we did in group this week

This week we talked about how important tone of voice can be in understanding the meaning of a statement and in determining the emotion of the person talking. We also played "Tone of Voice Jeopardy." In this game we guessed the tone of voice being used—happy, sad, mad, or neutral. We learned that tone of voice is different than the content of a statement. In fact, we practiced saying the same statement using different tones of voice.

What to work on at school

At school, you can encourage the child to pay special attention to the tone of voice teachers and students use, and encourage the child to guess the emotion that corresponds with the tone of voice the person used. You can also point out to the child that you can tell how he or she is feeling based on the tone of voice used. For example you could say, "I can tell you are feeling upset because you are using a mad tone of voice."

Session 6: Initiating conversations

Aim of session

The aim of this group session is to assist group members in learning how to initiate conversations with others and to learn appropriate chit-chat topics.

Empirical basis for the skill

Conversational skills are extensively discussed in the literature (Cragar and Horvath 2003; Howlin and Yates 1999; Marriage *et al.* 1995; Ozonoff and Miller 1995; Williams 1989). In addition, Heitzman-Powell (2003) specifically addresses the importance of learning how to appropriately initiate conversations.

Introduce initiating conversations

Group leaders should facilitate a discussion with group members regarding the importance of being able to initiate conversations. They should highlight that knowing how to start conversations is a skill that can help group members make friends.

Group leaders should facilitate a discussion with group members regarding how they think they should go about starting a conversation with someone. In addition, they should encourage group members to brainstorm "chit-chat" topics that could help them start talking with others. Some examples of "safe" chit-chat topics may include: school, homework, or popular movies.

Chit-Chat index cards and roleplays

Materials

- Index cards
- Writing utensils

Directions

Group leaders should divide the group into pairs and have them work together on creating chit-chat index cards. Group members should work with their partners on writing down "safe" chit-chat topics on their index cards. Each group member should make their own index card of chit-chat topics with the help of their partner. Time permitting, each group member should make two chit-chat index cards (they can be identical) in order to allow them to take one home and leave one at group.

Next, group leaders should explain to the group members that they will now practice making chit-chat with other group members. Group leaders should divide the group again into different pairs. Each group member will roleplay with at least two to three different group members. It is important that the group leaders facilitate these roleplays and provide feedback to the group members regarding their performance in the roleplays. If a pair has difficulty with a roleplay, the group leader should facilitate the pair trying the roleplay again. Furthermore, group leaders can use visual supports during the roleplays to remind group members of the basic component skills of conversations (i.e., look at the person who is talking).

The roleplays should include the group members practicing introducing themselves and then transitioning into chit-chat. They may use their index cards to help them remember topics they can discuss, but they should still fully engage in the conversation with the other person, making appropriate eye contact. Thus, the index cards can be glanced at to serve as a reminder but should not be stared at throughout the roleplay.

Once all group members have completed roleplays with two or three other group members, the members should meet as a group again. Group leaders should facilitate a discussion regarding the chit-chat topics that group members found to be most successful. Group members can also add new topics to their chit-chat index cards as they hear new ideas.

Snack and social time

During snack time, group members should be encouraged to practice chitchatting with other group members. As group leaders hear good chit-chat topics, they should reinforce group members and point out that they may want to add that topic to their index cards. Again, it is essential that group leaders facilitate this social snack time.

Closing

At the end of the session, group members should be encouraged to appropriately tell each other goodbye and that they will see each other again next week. If there are any special upcoming occasions (e.g., birthdays, vacations, holidays), group members should be encouraged to acknowledge them to one another. Distribute parent handouts to the parents and also provide parents with a copy of the teacher handout that they can share with their children's teachers.

Session 6: Initiating conversations

PARENT HANDOUT

What we did during group today

Today we learned about the importance of being able to "chit-chat" with others as a way to initiate conversations. We learned that being able to start conversations with others can help us make more friends and have more positive social experiences. We first made index cards with "safe" chit-chat topics on them to help us remember what is OK to talk about with others. Then we practiced both introducing ourselves to others and engaging in chit-chat by roleplaying with other group members.

What to work on at home

You can point out to your child when you are engaging in chit-chat to help your child gain more awareness of what chit-chat is and when to use it. For example, when your child comes home from school and you ask your child about his or her day, you can let him or her know that the two of you are chit-chatting. When the opportunity presents itself for chit-chat, such as when riding in the car together, you can encourage your child to start up a conversation with you. Provide feedback to your child about how well he or she is chit-chatting and provide suggestions as appropriate. For example, if your child always tries to start conversations with the same topic, suggest another topic to try.

Session 6: Initiating conversations

TEACHER HANDOUT

What we did in group this week

This week we learned about the importance of being able to "chit-chat" with others as a way to initiate conversations. We learned that being able to start conversations with others can help us make more friends and have more positive social experiences. We first made index cards with "safe" chit-chat topics on them to help us remember what is OK to talk about with others. Then we practiced both introducing ourselves to others and engaging in chit-chat by roleplaying with other group members.

What to work on at school

At school, you can encourage the child to engage in chit-chat with you before school or during other "downtimes" in your classroom. Provide feedback to the child about how well he or she is chit-chatting and provide suggestions as appropriate. For example, if the child always tries to start conversations with the same topic, suggest another topic to try. You can also encourage the child to start conversations with other students in the class. For example, you can provide an incentive for the child to introduce him or herself to two or three students at lunch or recess and chit-chat with them for a few minutes. It will be important, however, for you to facilitate these interactions in order to provide the child with a successful social experience.

Session 7: Maintaining conversations: Basic conversational skills

Aim of session

The aim of this group session is to assist group members in learning how to maintain conversations with others and to learn basic conversational skills.

Empirical basis for the skill

Conversational skills are well addressed in the literature (Cragar and Horvath 2003; Howlin and Yates 1999; Marriage *et al.* 1995; Ozonoff and Miller 1995; Williams 1989). Additionally, Heitzman-Powell (2003) specifically addresses the importance of learning how to maintain conversations. While initiating a conversation is an important skill to have, being able to sustain conversations is also very important. These are foundational skills to forming friendships with others.

Introduce maintaining conversations

Group leaders should remind group members that last week they learned how to start conversations, and tell them that this week they will work on how to keep conversations going. Group leaders should discuss with group members the importance of being able to keep conversations going and highlight that it is a foundational skill to developing friendships. Next, they should facilitate a discussion of how one should go about maintaining a conversation. For example, they could pose questions such as:

- How long should you talk?
- What should you talk about?
- What details should be included or not included?
- How will you be able to tell if the other person wants to talk?
- When should you ask a question?
- How can you be a good listener?
- How will you know the conversation is over?

Group leaders should assist group members in answering these questions. When discussing what to talk about with the other person, remind group members of the chit-chat topics they practiced last week. Also, encourage them to think about what they know about the other person and use that as a springboard for conversation. Remind them of the "Everyone Who" game that was played the first week of group and that they can use information they know about other group members from that game to help them know what to talk about in a conversation.

Group leaders should also review basic conversational skills with the group members. For example, they should discuss the importance of not talking in long monologues. Group leaders can help group members brainstorm how they will know if they have been talking too long. One example would be when the other person starts looking bored or distracted. Group leaders should help group members break this down into social cues that they can look for when in a conversation. For example, they would need to watch for the other person:

- fidgeting

- looking away (i.e., reducing eye contact)

- yawning

- trying to interrupt or say something.

Group leaders should also discuss the importance of including *some* details but not *all* the details of a story. Including too many details means that you will be talking too long in a conversation.

Group leaders should also discuss how to be a good listener and the skills that go along with being a good listener. Examples include:

- making eye contact

- making comments about what the other person said

- asking follow-up questions

- nodding your head while the other person is talking to indicate that you are listening.

Group leaders should also ask group members what they think they should do if a silence occurs in the conversation. Group leaders should facilitate this discussion and be sure to mention that they could:

- ask a related question

- make a related comment

- end the conversation if it has been going on for a few minutes.

With regard to ending the conversation, group leaders should review this skill with group members and discuss the need for a smooth transition (i.e., they should not just say goodbye and walk away). Group leaders should facilitate a discussion of good ending transitions. One example of an ending sequence would include: glancing at your watch, saying you have to get going soon, saying you enjoyed chatting with the other person, and saying goodbye.

Group leaders' roleplay

Given that these basic conversational skills do not have set rules (i.e., there is no set number of details you should or should not include), it will be important for the group members to have the opportunity to see some of these skills "in action." Two group leaders should roleplay a conversation while a third group leader will "freeze" the roleplay at key times to ask the group members about what they see going on in the roleplay.

The group leaders involved in the roleplay should demonstrate both good and poor social skills, especially those discussed at the beginning of group. They should begin, however, with displaying poor conversational skills. For example:

- talking too long while the other person shows signs of boredom

- silences

- including too many details

- making unrelated comments or asking unrelated questions.

When these poor conversational skills occur, the third group leader should "freeze" the conversation and ask the group members to point out what is not going well. The group leader should facilitate this discussion and then ask group members what the group leaders in the roleplay should do to "fix" the conversation. Then, the group leaders in the roleplay should "fix" that part of the conversation before moving on to display another poor conversational skill.

Once this first roleplay is over, the group leaders should roleplay another conversation, but this time displaying good conversational skills. Again, the third group leader should "freeze" the roleplay at key points and ask group members to comment on the skills they see the group leaders in the roleplay displaying.

Maintaining conversations roleplays

Group leaders should tell the group members that they will now have the opportunity to practice their conversational skills with other group members. The format is similar to the previous group session, except that the focus of the roleplays is on maintaining conversations. The roleplays should include initiating, maintaining, and ending a conversation.

Group leaders should divide the group into pairs. Each group member should roleplay with at least two to three different group members. Again, it is vital that the group leaders facilitate these roleplays and provide feedback to the group members regarding their performance in the roleplays. If a pair has difficulty with a roleplay, the group leader should facilitate the pair trying the roleplay again. In fact, group leaders can "freeze" the roleplay and ask the group members in the pair to brainstorm what could be done to "fix" the conversation. Furthermore, they can again use visual supports during the roleplays to remind group members of the basic component skills of conversations (i.e., look at the person who is talking).

Once all group members have completed roleplays with two or three other group members, they should meet as a group again. Group leaders should facilitate a discussion regarding how the conversations went and group members can share their experiences. Group members should be encouraged to share what helped them be successful with maintaining a conversation.

Snack and social time

During snack time, group members should be encouraged to practice both initiating and maintaining conversations with other group members. As group leaders hear good conversational skills, they should positively reinforce those group members. Again, it is essential that group leaders facilitate this social snack time.

Closing

At the end of the session, group members should be encouraged to transition into ending their conversations, as practiced in the roleplays earlier in the group session. They should be encouraged to appropriately tell each other goodbye and that they will see each other again next week. If there are any special upcoming occasions (e.g., birthdays, vacations, holidays), group members should be encouraged to acknowledge them to one another. Distribute parent handouts to the parents and also provide parents with a copy of the teacher handout that they can share with their children's teachers.

Session 7: Maintaining conversations: Basic conversational skills

PARENT HANDOUT

What we did during group today

Today we continued to talk about the importance of having good conversational skills. We learned that having good conversational skills can help us develop more friendships and have more positive social experiences. Today we focused on learning how to maintain conversations. We talked about the components of good conversational skills by asking questions such as:

- How long should you talk?
- What should you talk about?
- What details should be included or not included?
- How will you be able to tell if the other person wants to talk?
- When should you ask a question?
- How can you be a good listener?
- How will you know the conversation is over?

We practiced our conversational skills in roleplays and we even got to see our group leaders roleplay too! We "froze" our roleplays when poor conversational skills were being displayed and then talked about how to "fix" the conversation.

What to work on at home

You can practice conversational skills with your child by participating in a roleplay with him or her. In fact, you can display a poor conversational skill, "freeze" the roleplay, and then ask your child for help regarding how to "fix" the roleplay. For example, you could tell a story and talk in a long monologue without asking a question or pausing long enough for your child to comment. In addition, when you see your child demonstrating good conversational skills, positively reinforce him or her and say exactly what you liked about what he or she did. For example, if your child is talking for quite awhile, stops, and then asks you a good question, you can tell him or her, "I really like the way you realized you were talking for too long and asked me a good question. Great job!"

Session 7: Maintaining conversations: Basic conversational skills

TEACHER HANDOUT

What we did in group this week

This week we continued to talk about the importance of having good conversational skills. We learned that having good conversational skills can help us develop more friendships and have more positive social experiences. This week we focused on learning how to maintain conversations. We talked about the components of good conversational skills by asking questions such as:

- How long should you talk?
- What should you talk about?
- What details should be included or not included?
- How will you be able to tell if the other person wants to talk?
- When should you ask a question?
- How can you be a good listener?
- How will you know the conversation is over?

We practiced our conversational skills in roleplays and we even got to see our group leaders roleplay too! We "froze" our roleplays when poor conversational skills were being displayed and then talked about how to "fix" the conversation.

What to work on at school

At school, you can encourage the child to practice his or her conversational skills with you. Similar to the activity done in group this week, you could engage in a roleplay with the child in which you display a poor conversational skill, "freeze" the roleplay, and then ask him or her for help regarding how to "fix" the conversation. For example, you could tell a *very* detailed story (i.e., too many details), freeze the roleplay, and then ask the child how you should "fix" the conversation. In addition, when you see the child demonstrating good conversational skills, positively reinforce him or her and say exactly what you liked about what he or she did. For example, if the child is talking for quite awhile, stops, and then asks you a good question, you can tell him or her, "I really like the way you realized you were talking for too long and asked me a good question. Great job!"

Session 8: Maintaining conversations: Responding to the emotions of others

Aim of session

The aim of this group session is to assist group members in learning how to appropriately respond to the emotions of others within a conversation.

Empirical basis for the skill

As reviewed previously, conversational skills are discussed in the literature (Cragar and Horvath 2003; Heitzman-Powell 2003; Howlin and Yates 1999; Marriage *et al.* 1995; Ozonoff and Miller 1995; Williams 1989). In addition, emotional awareness is also a theme in the literature (Marriage *et al.* 1995; Mesibov 1985; Provencal 2003; Williams 1989). While these two areas may be thought about separately, they often interact in social situations. Thus, individuals often engage in conversations that have an emotional component to them.

Introduce emotion and conversation interplay

Group leaders should briefly remind group members of the skills they have learned over the past seven weeks, and should point out that the group members have learned about:

- emotions
- facial expressions
- varying degrees of emotions
- the importance of tone of voice
- initiating, maintaining, and ending conversations.

They should then explain to the group members that today they will have the opportunity to use all of the skills they have learned up to this point.

Group leaders should facilitate a discussion with group members regarding how emotion and conversational skills might interact with each other. For example, they can point out that sometimes people share news that has an emotion connected to it and ask group members to brainstorm some scenarios in which this might occur. Examples would include: when someone has a family member or pet die (sad), when someone gets a good grade on an exam (happy), or when someone has an argument with a parent or sibling (mad).

Group leaders should ask group members to discuss how they can determine the emotion the other person is feeling. This process would include:

- listening to what the person is saying
- looking at their facial expression
- listening to their tone of voice.

These three things can help determine the emotion of the other person.

Next, group leaders should facilitate a discussion regarding how group members think they should respond to someone who just shared good or bad news with them. If this is too abstract for group members, group leaders can pose specific situations and ask them to brainstorm appropriate responses. For example, they could ask them to pretend that they just got a call from a friend who said that their grandmother died. They can also ask specific questions about the scenarios such as:

- Should you ask details about how your friend's grandmother died? (answer: no)

- Should you ask your friend if there is anything you can do to help? (answer: yes)

- Should you abruptly change topics? (answer: no)

- Should you ignore what your friend said and tell your friend about what a great day you've had? (answer: no)

- Should you tell your friend that you are sorry to hear that his/her grandmother died? (answer: yes)

Group leaders should pose a few different scenarios to the group and ask specific questions about those scenarios in order to help group members think about what they should and should not say when responding to the given scenario.

Introduce roleplays

Group leaders should tell group members that they will now have the opportunity to practice responding to someone who is sharing emotional news with them. They should explain that the roleplays will be a bit different this time in that each group member will roleplay with a group leader in front of the group. The group leaders will be the ones sharing the news and the group members will roleplay how to respond. Group leaders will be pretending that they are peers of the group members. Examples of scenarios are outlined below. Group leaders can draw a scenario out of a container and perform the one they drew.

If a roleplay is not going well, a group leader not participating in the roleplay can "freeze" the roleplay and ask the group members watching to offer positive suggestions to the group member in the roleplay. Once each roleplay is completed, group leaders should ask the group members who watched the roleplay to point out the good things they saw happening in the roleplay. Group leaders should also pose questions to the group members who watched, such as, "_____ did a great job! What are some other ways we could respond to the same scenario?" It is important to have group members brainstorm a number of appropriate ways to respond to the same scenario so that when they encounter similar situations, they will have a number of options from which to choose.

Roleplay scenarios

1. You just found out that you got an "A" on your math test!

2. You argued with one of your good friends.

3. You were called bad names on the bus ride home from school today.

4. Your parents just told you that your next vacation will be to Disney World, a place you've always wanted to visit.

5. You lost your favorite toy/video game today.

6. You have a big test coming up tomorrow.

7. You just found out that your pet dog was hit by a car.

8. You just found out that your family is getting a pool!

Snack and social time

During snack time, group members should be encouraged to sustain longer conversations with other group members. Similar to last week, as group leaders hear good conversational skills, they should positively reinforce those group members. Group members should also be encouraged to pay particular attention to any emotions that come up during their conversations and respond appropriately to those emotions. As always, it is essential that group leaders facilitate this social snack time.

Closing

At the end of the session, group members should be encouraged to transition into ending their conversations, as practiced last week. They should also be encouraged to appropriately tell each other goodbye and that they will see each other again next week. If there are any special upcoming occasions (e.g., birthdays, vacations, holidays), group members should be encouraged to acknowledge them to one another. Distribute parent handouts to the parents and also provide parents with a copy of the teacher handout that they can share with their children's teachers.

Session 8: Maintaining conversations: Responding to the emotions of others

PARENT HANDOUT

What we did during group today

Today we talked about how emotions can come up in our conversations with others and that we need to know how to respond to those emotions. We practiced how to respond to people when they are feeling sad, mad, happy, anxious and more! We talked about what to say, what not to say, and how to be supportive of the other person. We even had the chance to roleplay with our group leaders! When any of us got "stuck" in a roleplay, we helped each other think of ways to respond.

What to work on at home

At home, try roleplaying situations which involve different feelings with your child. You can continue to practice ways to respond. You can also talk with your child about what is an appropriate way to respond and what might not be so helpful. Encourage him or her to think of a few different ways to respond to the same situation. In addition, you can talk with your child about times you have experienced various emotions and share with him or her what types of responses from others were helpful.

✓

TEACHER HANDOUT

What we did in group this week

This week we talked about how emotions can come up in our conversations with others and that we need to know how to respond to those emotions. We practiced how to respond to people when they are feeling sad, mad, happy, anxious and more! We talked about what to say, what not to say, and how to be supportive of the other person. We even had the chance to roleplay with our group leaders! When any of us got "stuck" in a roleplay, we helped each other think of ways to respond.

What to work on at school

At school, you can roleplay situations with the child that involve different feelings. For example, you can roleplay someone telling a friend about good or bad news they recently received. You can talk with the child about appropriate ways to respond and encourage him or her to think of a few different ways to respond to the same situation. In addition, when a situation presents itself in the school setting, you can point out that you noticed *(name)* _____ is feeling *(emotion)* _____ and suggest that the child try talking to that person. For example, you could say "I noticed that Julie is feeling upset because she lost her homework. Let's go check and see how she is doing." It will be important for you to facilitate this interaction in order to foster a successful social interaction.

Session 9: Conversational skills: Phone skills

Aim of session

The aim of this group session is to teach group members basic phone skills, highlighting the importance of paying special attention to tone of voice, because on the phone there are no visual cues on which to rely.

Empirical basis for the skill

Conversational skills are well discussed in the literature (Cragar and Horvath 2003; Heitzman-Powell 2003; Howlin and Yates 1999; Marriage *et al.* 1995; Ozonoff and Miller 1995; Williams 1989). In addition, emotional awareness is an area that is discussed in the literature (Mesibov 1985; Marriage *et al.* 1995; Provencal 2003; Williams 1989). Furthermore, tone of voice is specifically addressed in the literature (Barnhill *et al.* 2002). All of these skill areas play a role in phone skills. Talking on the phone requires good conversational skills, emotion awareness, and the ability to accurately interpret tone of voice.

Introduce phone skills

Group leaders should discuss with group members the importance of having good phone skills. The phone is a means by which we communicate with people who may live far away from us and is a way for us to talk to people when we cannot meet with them in person. Group leaders should point out that many times we are invited to do things over the phone and that we often get news, good or bad, over the phone from friends and family. They should highlight that having good phone skills is important in a friendship, because friends often talk on the phone together and invite one another to do things by using the phone.

Group leaders should encourage group members to briefly share a time that they have spoken on the phone with someone. They should highlight that many different types of conversations occur on the phone such as:

- invitations to do something
- sharing good news
- sharing bad news
- asking a question about something (i.e., a question about a homework assignment)
- just chit-chatting.

Next, they should facilitate a discussion with group members regarding what they think is important to remember when talking on the phone, and ensure that listening for tone of voice is discussed, especially given that on the phone, group members cannot rely on facial expressions to help them. Other things to remember include:

- how to handle silences

- how to start, maintain, and end a conversation

- how to respond to someone else's emotion.

Group leaders should briefly review these skills with the group members, encouraging them to call upon what they have learned in previous group sessions.

In addition, group leaders should facilitate a discussion with group members regarding appropriate ways to answer the phone and the importance of engaging in some chit-chat before diving into the purpose of the phone call. The mock phone calls that will be used later in the group session can serve as examples. For example, group members can point out that if you have a question about a homework assignment, you should not just say hello and then ask the question; it is important to ask how the other person is doing or how his or her day has been. Group leaders should also discuss with group members how to end a phone conversation appropriately.

Mock phone calls

Group leaders should explain to group members that they will be making mock phone calls to one another and that the topics of conversation will vary. Group leaders should divide group members into pairs and change pairs for each mock phone call. Each group member should also have ample opportunity to be both the person initiating the phone call and the person answering the phone call.

Each pair should have a group leader present to facilitate the mock phone call. Additionally, each pair should roleplay the same scenario simultaneously. Given that the group members will be roleplaying simultaneously, group leaders may wish to place each pair in a separate room to reduce the amount of background noise. Potential topics of the phone conversations are listed below. The initial phone calls should be simple in nature and cover topics such as asking a question about homework. The subsequent topics should become more complex. It is helpful to use topics with which group members have already had experience and practice.

Mock phone call topics

Simple

- Asking a question about homework—what is the math homework assignment for tonight?

- Asking a question about an upcoming event at school—what day is the field trip to the museum?

- Asking a question about when something is due—when is the book report due?

More complex

- Inviting a friend over to play.
- Inviting a friend to go to a movie with you.
- A friend calls with good news—he or she got an "A" on the math test today.

Most complex

- A friend calls with bad news—a relative died.
- A friend calls just to chat.
- A friend calls because he or she is nervous about a test tomorrow.

Group members should sit in chairs, back-to-back so that they cannot look at each other's facial expressions. As in previous groups, if the mock phone call is going poorly, the group leader can "freeze" the phone call and work with the pair on how to "fix" the call. Then, the pair can try the phone call again.

If your particular facility permits, "actual phone calls" can be made between group members once every group member has completed a few mock phone calls. It is important that a group leader be with each person on the phone in case they get "stuck" during the call. Considering next week is the last group and the group will be going out to dinner together, group leaders can instruct the group members to call one another and invite them to dinner next week for their "actual call."

Following the "actual calls" the group members can meet as a group again and briefly discuss how their phone conversations went. Group leaders should encourage group members to talk about what helped them have successful phone conversations.

Snack and social time

During snack time, group members should continue to be encouraged to sustain longer conversations with other group members. As group leaders hear good conversational skills, they should positively reinforce those group members. Again, it is essential that group leaders facilitate this social snack time. In addition, group leaders should remind group members that next week is the last week of group. And let group members know that they will all be going out to dinner together next week to celebrate. If there are any decisions to be made about next week, such as where to go to eat, these should be decided during snack time.

Closing

At the end of the session, group members should be encouraged to transition into ending their conversations, as practiced last week. They should also be encouraged to appropriately tell each other goodbye and that they will see each other again next week. If there are any special upcoming occasions (e.g., birthdays, vacations, holidays), they should be encouraged to acknowledge them to one another. Distribute parent handouts to the parents and also provide parents with a copy of the teacher handout that they can share with their children's teachers. Remind parents that next week is the last week of group and let them know that the group will be going out to eat together to celebrate. Also, ask parents if they have any objection to their child participating in a phone number exchange during next week's group—this is a way group members can stay in touch and continue any newly made friendships after group ends.

Session 9: Conversational Skills: Phone skills

PARENT HANDOUT

What we did during group today

Today we worked on our phone skills! We did this by having mock phone calls with other group members. We talked on the phone about many things, such as asking a question about homework, inviting someone over, and sharing good or bad news with someone. We had to rely on all the skills we have learned in group so far. We had to remember to pay special attention to tone of voice and all of our conversational skills. At the end of group, we got to actually call a fellow group member and invite him or her to go to dinner next week!

What to work on at home

At home, try roleplaying mock phone calls with your child. In fact, if you have a cell phone or second line, try calling your child and having a conversation with him or her on the phone. You can pretend to be calling to invite your child to do something, to be asking a homework question, or to share some news. Talk with your child about how the conversation went and the specific phone skills you heard him or her use. You can also encourage your child to call a relative or friend of the family so that he or she can continue to practice phone skills.

REMINDER: NEXT WEEK IS OUR LAST WEEK OF GROUP. WE WILL BE GOING OUT TO DINNER AS A GROUP TO CELEBRATE, SO LEAVE DINNER TO US NEXT WEEK!

Also, we would like to encourage the group members to exchange phone numbers with one another at the end of group so that they can continue the friendships they have made in group outside of group. If you would not like your child to exchange phone numbers, please let a group leader know. Thank you!

✓

Session 9: Conversational Skills: Phone skills

TEACHER HANDOUT

What we did in group this week

This week we worked on our phone skills! We did this by having mock phone calls with other group members. We talked on the phone about many things, such as asking a question about homework, inviting someone over, and sharing good or bad news with someone. We had to rely on all the skills we have learned in group so far. We had to remember to pay special attention to tone of voice and all of our conversational skills. Since next week is our last group and we will be going out to dinner to celebrate, we got to actually call a fellow group member and invite him or her to go to dinner next week!

What to work on at school

At school, students generally do not talk on the phone, but you can help the child prepare for phone conversations! For example, you can help the child think about who in the class to call if he or she has a question about homework or something else school-related. You can help him or her choose someone who will encourage a positive social interaction on the phone.

REMINDER: NEXT WEEK IS THE LAST WEEK OF GROUP!

Session 10: Manners and dinner outing

Aim of session

The aim of this group session is to teach group members basic manners when dining out for a meal, to practice their conversational skills in a naturalistic setting, and to celebrate the end of group.

Empirical basis for the skill

The issue of generalization of social skills is discussed in the literature (Cragar and Horvath 2003; Heitzman-Powell 2003; Howlin and Yates 1999; Marriage *et al.* 1995). In order to improve generalization of skills taught, community outings were used in a number of groups specifically designed for children and adolescents on the autism spectrum (Barnhill *et al.* 2002; Mesibov 1984; Ozonoff and Miller 1995; Provencal 2003).

Introduce manners

Group leaders should facilitate a discussion with group members regarding the manners they will need to keep in mind during the dinner outing this group session. They should point out that using good manners shows others respect and consideration and can help maintain friendships. Group leaders should assist group members with discussing what they should remember on the way to and from dinner, such as: chit-chatting with others, staying with the group, and talking with a few different group members. Group members should be encouraged to think about what they would like to order at the restaurant, as they will be ordering their own meals, although group leaders should be available to assist. Group members should discuss that they will need to look directly at the person who will take their orders, speak clearly, and be ready to answer questions regarding their meal orders.

With regard to manners at the restaurant, group leaders should ensure that key manners are discussed, such as:

- maintaining conversations with other group members
- choosing appropriate conversational topics (i.e., not a gruesome topic)
- not interrupting others
- remembering when to stop talking and when to ask someone else a question
- not chewing with a mouth full of food
- excusing themselves if they need to leave the table (i.e., to go to the restroom)
- eating neatly

- using a napkin
- appropriately using silverware.

Group leaders should address other manners that are specific to the place the group will dine.

Dinner outing

Group leaders should facilitate the social interactions that occur during the outing. For example, they should assist group members with conversation topics if group members get "stuck," and also discreetly and directly help group members remember their manners if they are engaging in inappropriate behavior.

Phone number exchange

Once the group has returned from the dinner outing, group leaders should encourage group members to exchange phone numbers with other group members so that they can continue their friendships outside of group, of course taking into consideration any parents who do not want their children to participate in this activity. Group leaders should facilitate this interaction and provide coaching to group members as they ask other group members for their phone numbers.

Closing

At the end of the session, group members should be encouraged to appropriately tell each other goodbye, as well as the group leaders. Group leaders should facilitate these goodbyes. Distribute parent handouts to the parents and also provide parents with a copy of the teacher handout that they can share with their children's teachers. Group leaders should also let parents know with whom their children exchanged phone numbers so that parents can facilitate and encourage their children to contact them.

Session 10: Manners and dinner outing

PARENT HANDOUT

What we did during group today

Today we worked on our manners. We discussed what manners are and that using good manners shows others respect and consideration. We specifically talked about manners related to dining out. We talked about many manners, including choosing appropriate topics of table conversation, chewing with our mouths closed, maintaining social interaction with those seated with us, and using a napkin. We then had the opportunity to practice our manners when we went out to dinner together. We also had the chance to practice ordering our own meals.

What to work on at home

At home, remind your child to use good manners, especially those related to mealtimes. When your child demonstrates good manners, positively reinforce him or her and state exactly what you saw and liked. For example, you could say, "I really liked how you used your napkin to wipe off your mouth," or "I liked how you excused yourself from the table before leaving the table." Also, you can encourage your child to practice his or her conversational skills at the dinner table including encouraging your child to appropriately initiate, maintain, and end a conversation and choosing topics appropriate for dinner table conversation.

THANKS FOR A GREAT GROUP!

✓

Session 10: Manners and dinner outing

TEACHER HANDOUT

What we did in group this week

This week we worked on our manners. We discussed what manners are and that using good manners shows others respect and consideration. We specifically talked about manners related to dining out. We talked about many manners, including choosing appropriate topics of table conversation, chewing with our mouths closed, maintaining social interaction with those seated with us, and using a napkin. We then had the opportunity to practice our manners when we went out to dinner together. We also had the chance to practice ordering our own meals.

What to work on at school

At school, you can remind the child to use good manners, especially at lunch and/or snack time. When the child demonstrates good manners, positively reinforce him or her and state exactly what you saw and liked. For example, you could say, "I really liked how you chewed with your mouth closed," or "I liked how you waited until you were done chewing before talking."

Since this week was the last week of group, encourage the child to use *all* of the social skills he or she has learned throughout the past ten weeks at school!

THANKS FOR A GREAT GROUP!

8. Supplemental Sessions

Supplemental Session Topics

Supplemental Session 1: Emotion collages

Supplemental Session 2: Tone of voice movie clips

Supplemental Session 3: Joining a group

Supplemental Session 4: Being a good sport

Supplemental Session 5: Personal space

Supplemental Session 6: Friendship skills

Supplemental Session 7: Perspective-taking and empathy

Supplemental Session 8: Flexibility and adaptability

Supplemental Session 9: Politeness

Supplemental Session 10: Understanding sarcasm and figures of speech

Adolescent Supplemental Session 1: Hanging out

Adolescent Supplemental Session 2: School dances

Adolescent Supplemental Session 3: Interviewing skills

The following supplemental sessions are provided in order to allow the number of groups to be extended. In addition, these supplemental groups can be used if the group members have already learned some of the basic skills and other group session topics and activities are needed. Furthermore, if the group members have an area of difficulty, the supplemental sessions can be added to support acquisition of that skill. For example, if the group members are having difficulty identifying the emotions of others, Supplemental Session 1: Emotion collages could be added to the group session sequence.

Three adolescent supplemental sessions have also been included to address topics that are specific to teens with Asperger's Syndrome (AS). These sessions should only be added after the ten basic, foundational sessions have been completed. In order for the group members to be able to successfully learn the skills in the adolescent supplemental sessions, the foundational skills need to have been covered already. For example, in order for the group members to be able to successfully learn about hanging out with friends, they need to have already covered emotion awareness, conversational skills, chit-chat, phone skills, and so forth. These foundational skills are component skills to hanging out with friends, a more complex skill.

Supplemental Session 1: Emotion collages

Aim of session

The aim of this group session is to facilitate awareness of basic emotions among group members.

Empirical basis for the skill

Emotional awareness is well discussed in the literature (Marriage *et al.* 1995; Mesibov 1985; Provencal 2003; Williams 1989). More specifically, identifying facial expressions is a component skill of correctly identifying emotions in others, a skill addressed by Barnhill and colleagues (2002).

Introduce emotions

Group leaders should facilitate a discussion of the basic emotions people feel, if this has not been previously covered. Examples include: happy, sad, mad, and scared. Group leaders should ask group members to discuss how they are able to know what others are feeling, and make sure the topic of facial expression is covered. They should also discuss the importance of being able to accurately identify the emotions of others. They should highlight that being able to read others' facial expressions helps us know how others are feeling, which helps us know how to approach or respond to others. As a result, being able to identify the emotions of others fosters positive social interactions with others.

Introduce identifying emotions in pictures

Group leaders should facilitate a discussion regarding what cues to look for in a picture to identify how someone is feeling. They can present a picture to the group in order to stimulate discussion. They should ensure that the facial characteristics of the four basic emotions are covered (i.e., happy, sad, mad, and scared). For example, for a sad facial expression, facial cues would include the corners of the mouth being down turned, the eyebrows moving closer together, a downward eye gaze, and possibly the presence of tears.

Emotion collages

Group leaders should tell the group members that they will be making emotion collages in small groups (see below). Depending upon the number of members in the group, group leaders should divide the group members into groups of two or three, creating a total of four groups. Each group should be assigned one of the four basic emotions (i.e., happy, sad, mad, and scared).

Emotion collages

Materials
- Child-appropriate magazines
- Scissors
- Poster board
- Markers
- Glue

Directions
Group members should first write their assigned emotion somewhere on their poster board. They should work within their established groups to find pictures in the magazine that represent the emotion they were assigned. For example, if a group was assigned "sad" as their emotion, they should look for pictures in the magazines of people who look sad. They should cut out these pictures and glue them on their poster board, creating a collage of the emotion they were assigned. Group leaders should facilitate social interactions during this time, assisting with conflict resolution and chit-chat among group members while they work together on the collages.

Once group members have completed their collages, they should meet as a group to share their collages with one another. Group leaders should facilitate each group displaying their emotion collage to the rest of the group. Group leaders should encourage group members to teach the group about the emotion they were assigned, by pointing out the facial cues of their assigned emotion within the pictures on their collage. After each group has presented their collage, group leaders should present a few pictures to the group and have them guess the emotion of the person in the picture. Again, group members should be encouraged to point out the facial cues that led them to guess the correct emotion.

Snack and social time
During snack time, group members should be encouraged to pay special attention to the facial expressions of group members and use facial cues to determine others' emotions. Again, it is essential that group leaders facilitate social interactions during snack time.

Closing
At the end of the session, group members should be encouraged to appropriately tell each other goodbye and that they will see each other again next week. If there are any special upcoming occasions (e.g., birthdays, vacations, holidays), they should be encouraged to acknowledge them to one another. Distribute parent handouts to the parents and also provide parents with a copy of the teacher handout that they can share with their children's teachers.

✓

Supplemental Session 1: Emotion collages

PARENT HANDOUT

What we did during group today

Today we talked about basic emotions, such as happy, mad, sad, and scared. We discussed how being able to figure out the emotions of others can help us have positive social interactions. We worked in small groups with other group members to make emotion collages. We cut out pictures from magazines that represented these emotions and presented our collages to the group. We focused on how we can determine others' emotions by looking at their facial expressions. We specifically talked about the facial cues that correspond with each of the basic emotions.

What to work on at home

You can practice identifying emotions with your child by asking him or her to guess the emotions of people pictured in magazines or in photographs you have in your home. Talk with your child about the facial cues in the pictures that help determine the emotion of the person pictured. For example, if the person in the picture is happy, point out facial cues, such as a smile.

Supplemental Session 1: Emotion collages

TEACHER HANDOUT

What we did in group this week

This week we talked about basic emotions, such as happy, mad, sad, and scared. We discussed how being able to figure out the emotions of others can help us have positive social interactions. We worked in small groups with other group members to make emotion collages. We cut out pictures from magazines that represented these emotions and presented our collages to the group. We focused on how we can determine others' emotions by looking at their facial expressions. We specifically talked about the facial cues that correspond with each of the basic emotions.

What to work on at school

At school, you can have the child guess the emotions of people in posters or pictures within your classroom. Talk with the child about the facial cues in the pictures that help determine the emotion of the person pictured. For example, if the person in the picture is sad, point out facial cues, such as a frown.

Supplemental Session 2: Tone of voice movie clips

Aim of session

The aim of this group session is to further assist group members in being able to determine the emotions of others solely by listening to the tone of voice used.

Empirical basis for the skill

Identifying and expressing emotions is a theme in the literature (Marriage *et al.* 1995; Mesibov 1985; Provencal 2003; Williams 1989). In addition, Barnhill and colleagues (2002) specifically discuss the role that tone of voice plays in understanding the meaning of statements and in determining emotion. Lindner and Rosén (in press) found that children with AS have great difficulty accurately determining the emotions of others relying solely on tone of voice.

Introduce tone of voice

Group leaders should facilitate a discussion of the role tone of voice plays in determining the emotion of the person speaking, pointing out that listening to others' tones of voice helps us know how others are feeling, which helps us interact with others socially. They should make a few statements in varying tones of voice and have group members guess the emotion. It is important that the content of the statements made match the emotion. Group leaders should then ask group members what other hints or cues they should look for when trying to guess the emotion of others. They should highlight that group members should listen for tone of voice and also pay attention to the content of what the person is saying. The content of the statement is also a clue to the emotion the person is feeling.

Tone of voice movie clips

Group leaders should introduce the activity for this week to the group members (see below), and explain that the group members will be divided into small groups of two or three and will work with a group leader on identifying the emotions of characters in movies.

Tone of voice movie clips

Materials

- TVs
- VCRs/DVD players
- Movie clips

Directions

Prior to the start of group, group leaders should select clips from appropriate movies that demonstrate a particular emotion through tone of voice. An alternative is having group leaders tape record themselves making statements in varying tones of voice. Regardless, it is important that the content of the statements made in the movie clips or in the statements group leaders record matches the tone of voice.

One group leader should be with each small group of group members. If movie clips are being used, the TV should be turned around so that the group members cannot see the screen. Group members should be instructed to listen carefully to the movie clip or recorded statement and determine the emotion of the person speaking. The group leader with each small group should facilitate a discussion among the group members as they try to determine the emotion within the movie clip or recorded statement. If needed, the movie clip or recorded statement can be replayed a few times. Group leaders should facilitate the group members discussing both the tone of voice of the statement and the content of the statement in determining the emotion of the person or character speaking. Once group members determine the correct emotion of the movie clip or recorded statement, the group leader should present the next movie clip or recorded statement.

Snack and social time

During snack time, group members should be encouraged to talk with other group members, paying close attention to both the tone of voice of others and the content of what others are saying to determine the emotion. Group leaders should facilitate this and point out to group members how both their tone of voice and content of their statements help others know how they are feeling.

Closing

At the end of the session, group members should be encouraged to appropriately tell each other goodbye and that they will see each other again next week. If there are any special upcoming occasions (e.g., birthdays, vacations, holidays), they should be encouraged to acknowledge them to one another. Distribute parent handouts to the parents and also provide parents with a copy of the teacher handout that they can share with their children's teachers.

Supplemental Session 2: Tone of voice movie clips

PARENT HANDOUT

What we did during group today

Today we learned the importance of listening to the tone of voice others use and the content of their statements to help us figure out how others are feeling. We learned that being able to do this can help us know how to approach and interact with others. We talked about how both tone of voice and content of statements are important clues in determining the emotions of others. We practiced listening to both the tone of voice and the content of statements to determine emotions by listening to (not watching) movie clips and guessing the emotion of the person talking.

What to work on at home

You can practice with your child paying attention to the tone of voice of others and the content of their statements to figure out the emotion they are feeling. One way to do this is to have your child close his or her eyes while watching TV or a movie together and guess the emotion of the person talking. You can also make statements to your child and have him or her guess the emotion you are feeling based on what you said (content) and how you said it (tone of voice).

Supplemental Session 2: Tone of voice movie clips

TEACHER HANDOUT

What we did in group this week

This week we learned the importance of listening to the tone of voice others use and the content of their statements to help us figure out how others are feeling. We learned that being able to do this can help us know how to approach and interact with others. We talked about how both tone of voice and content of statements are important clues in determining the emotions of others. We practiced listening to both tone of voice and content of statements to determine emotions by listening to (not watching) movie clips and guessing the emotion of the person talking.

What to work on at school

At school, you can talk with the child about paying close attention to both what others are saying (content) and how they are saying it (tone of voice) to figure out how others are feeling. One way to practice this in the school setting is to have the child close his or her eyes while you make some statements and have him or her guess the emotion you are feeling. You can also ask the child to state how other students or teachers are feeling by listening to the tone of voice used and the content of their statements.

Supplemental Session 3: Joining a group

Aim of session

The aim of this group session is to help group members recognize social cues from others that can help them join a group of peers already engaged in an activity (i.e., playing a game, talking).

Empirical basis for the skill

Successfully joining a group of peers already involved in an activity requires a number of social skills. It requires an ability to read the body language and other nonverbal cues of others, a topic well discussed in the literature (Howlin and Yates 1999; Marriage *et al.* 1995; Ozonoff and Miller 1995; Williams 1989). In addition, successfully joining a group also requires good conversational skills, including being able to initiate and maintain conversations, another topic addressed in the literature (Cragar and Horvath 2003; Heitzman-Powell 2003; Howlin and Yates 1999; Marriage *et al.* 1995; Ozonoff and Miller 1995; Provencal 2003; Williams 1989). Furthermore, Cragar and Horvath (2003) specifically address group entry skills.

Introduce joining a group

Group leaders should discuss with the group the importance of being able to join a group of peers, pointing out that having this skill can increase their social interactions with others. They should then facilitate a discussion regarding how to join a group of people already engaged in an activity together. They should ask group members to think about what social cues they should look for when approaching a group of peers engaged in an activity. Examples include:

- Look for the person you know best.

- Look for an open physical space in the group.

- Make eye contact with the person you know best.

- Watch for any nonverbal invitations such as eye contact, someone waving you over to the group, or someone smiling at you.

Group leaders should then ask group members to describe how they think they should go about joining a group of peers engaged in an activity, and facilitate this discussion, ensuring that particular issues are covered. They should point out that group members should identify the person they know best in the group of peers already engaged in an activity and to also look for an open physical space near that person. Group members should approach the group near the person they know best and try to make eye contact with that person. While doing this, they should look for nonverbal invitations from anyone within the group. Once near the group, they should initiate some chit-chat with the person they know best by stating something such as, "Hi (<u>name</u>), what are you guys doing?" If the group of peers is involved in a conversation, the group member should use his or her conversational skills to maintain a conversation. If the group of peers is involved in a game, he or she should still use his or her conversational skills to engage in some brief chit-chat with those in the group and also ask an appropriate question about joining the game, such as, "Can I play the winner?" or "Can I play in the next round?"

Group leaders should also highlight for group members what they can do when they are engaged in an activity with a group of peers to encourage someone approaching the group to join them. Examples include:

- Make eye contact with the person.

- Smile at the person.

- Wave the person over toward the group.

- Initiate a conversation with the person.

Joining a group "frozen" roleplays

Group leaders should explain to group members that they will be playing a board game together while one group member leaves the room and then tries to join the group. One or more group leaders should help facilitate the game being played, and one group leader should be with the group member who will be attempting to join the group. Each group member should have the opportunity to be the person trying to join the other group members playing the board game.

The group leader helping the person trying to join the game should "freeze" the group playing the game and coach the person trying to join the game. For example, they should ask the person trying to join the game who they know best, where an open space is, what nonverbal invitations they may or may not see, and so forth. Then, the group leader should "unfreeze" the game and coach and facilitate the person trying to join the group to do so successfully. The group leaders who are facilitating the game can encourage the group members, at times, to demonstrate nonverbal invitations to the person trying to join the group.

Snack and social time

During snack time, group members should be encouraged to try and join in others' conversations appropriately, looking for social cues to help them do so successfully. They can also practice their conversational skills, especially with regard to initiating and maintaining conversations. Again, group leaders should facilitate these social interactions to ensure success.

Closing

At the end of the session, group members should be encouraged to appropriately tell each other goodbye and that they will see each other again next week. If there are any special upcoming occasions (e.g., birthdays, vacations, holidays), they should be encouraged to acknowledge them to one another. Distribute parent handouts to the parents and also provide parents with a copy of the teacher handout that they can share with their children's teachers.

Supplemental Session 3: Joining a group

PARENT HANDOUT

What we did during group today

Today we learned about the importance of being able to join a group of people already engaged in an activity, such as playing a game or talking together. We talked about how being able to join a group successfully will help us have more social interactions with others and can help us make more friends. We practiced joining a group of people engaged in an activity by playing a board game as a group and then taking turns trying to join the group. We talked about the social cues we should keep in mind when trying to join a group, such as:

- looking for the person we know best

- making eye contact with that person

- looking for an open physical space in the group

- watching for nonverbal invitations from others (i.e., someone smiling at you).

What to work on at home

At home, you can help your child practice these skills by playing a game with family members or friends and encouraging your child to join the group. You can coach your child by reminding him or her to look for important social cues. You can also "freeze" the situation and ask your child to explain to you what social cues are present to help him or her successfully join the group.

✓

Supplemental Session 3: Joining a group

TEACHER HANDOUT

What we did in group this week

This week we learned about the importance of being able to join a group of people already engaged in an activity, such as playing a game or talking together. We talked about how being able to join a group successfully will help us have more social interactions with others and can help us make more friends. We practiced joining a group of people engaged in an activity by playing a board game as a group and then taking turns trying to join the group. We talked about the social cues we should keep in mind when trying to join a group, such as:

- looking for the person we know best

- making eye contact with that person

- looking for an open physical space in the group

- watching for nonverbal invitations from others (i.e., someone smiling at you).

What to work on at school

At school, you can help the child practice joining a group of peers already engaged in an activity. A good place to practice these skills is at recess or other "downtime" at school. You can coach the child by helping the child think about the social cues he or she notices. You can also help the child choose which group to join, setting him or her up for a successful social interaction. You can help the child think about how to approach the group and what to say, and then you can help facilitate the child joining the group.

Supplemental Session 4: Being a good sport

Aim of session

The aim of this group session is to teach group members how to be a good sport, including conflict resolution skills, being supportive of other players, and knowing how to lose.

Empirical basis for the skill

A number of studies have used games or other recreational activities as a teaching technique (Barnhill *et al.* 2002; Howlin and Yates 1999; Marriage *et al.* 1995; Ozonoff and Miller 1995; Provencal 2003; Williams 1989). In order to successfully engage in group games or activities, individuals must know how to be a good sport. Thus, being a good sport is important in knowing how to interact with others, especially when engaging in organized games/sports.

Introduce being a good sport

Group leaders should facilitate a discussion with group members regarding the importance of being a good sport. They should indicate that being a good sport is important in being able to make and keep friendships, pointing out that others do not like to play with people who are not good sports. They should then facilitate a discussion what being a good sport means. Examples include:

- encouraging others to do their best (even if they are not on your team)
- congratulating others when they win
- making encouraging statements to others when they lose
- being ready for your turn
- staying calm when you or your team lose
- not bragging when you or your team wins
- accepting "calls" made by the person refereeing the game.

Group leaders should then pose scenarios to the group and facilitate group members brainstorming how they should respond. For example, they could ask group members to talk about how they should respond if:

- you just lost a game and you really wanted to win
- the person refereeing the game made a call that you don't agree with
- a fellow player has been trying really hard to do well but is having a difficult time
- you just won a game.

Group leaders can ask group members to briefly roleplay some of these scenarios with other group members, time permitting.

Being a good sport

Group leaders should organize a game for the group members to play together. Depending upon the season and the weather, the group can play an indoor game (e.g., a board game) or an outdoor game (e.g., kickball, softball). Throughout the game, group members should be reminded to be good sports. For example, when one person or team wins, that person should be prompted to make an appropriate statement to the other players, and the other players should be prompted to make an appropriate statement to the winner or winning team. It is essential that group leaders facilitate the game and prompt group members to use the skills they have learned to help them be good sports.

Snack and social time

During snack time, group members should be encouraged to chat with one another and learn more about each other. They could also be encouraged to talk about the games they enjoy playing, looking for common interests. Again, group leaders should facilitate these social interactions.

Closing

At the end of the session, group members should be encouraged to appropriately tell each other goodbye and that they will see each other again next week. If there are any special upcoming occasions (e.g., birthdays, vacations, holidays), they should be encouraged to acknowledge them to one another. Distribute parent handouts to the parents and also provide parents with a copy of the teacher handout that they can share with their children's teachers.

Supplemental Session 4: Being a good sport

PARENT HANDOUT

What we did during group today

Today we talked about the importance of being a "good sport" and that being a good sport can help us make and keep friends. We learned about things we can do to help us be good sports such as:

- encourage others to do their best
- accept the "calls" of the person refereeing the game
- congratulate the winner(s)
- react calmly if we lose.

We had the opportunity to practice being good sports by playing a game with the other group members.

What to work on at home

At home, you can help your child practice being a good sport by playing a game with your child and reminding him or her to demonstrate the skills he or she learned in group to be a good sport. You can also organize a game with other family members or friends in the neighborhood and you can help facilitate these interactions. Tell your child when you see him or her being a good sport! For example, you can say, "I liked how you stayed calm and congratulated the winner of the game when you lost the game."

✓

Supplemental Session 4: Being a good sport

TEACHER HANDOUT

What we did in group this week

This week we talked about the importance of being a "good sport" and that being a good sport can help us make and keep friends. We learned about things we can do to help us be good sports such as:

- encourage others to do their best
- accept the "calls" of the person refereeing the game
- congratulate the winner(s)
- react calmly if we lose.

We had the opportunity to practice being good sports by playing a game with the other group members.

What to work on at school

At school, you can help the child practice being a good sport at opportune times, such as during recess or other times during the day when the students engage in organized games or sports. For example, at recess, you can remind the child to be a good sport and you can facilitate this process. Tell the child when you see him or her being a good sport! For example, you can say, "I really liked how you accepted the call of the referee" or "I liked how you congratulated the winning team when your team lost."

Supplemental Session 5: Personal space

Aim of session

The aim of this group session is to increase group members' awareness of personal space and help them determine the personal space boundaries of others.

Empirical basis for the skill

The issue of personal space is related to body language, a topic discussed by Howlin and Yates (1999). Being able to determine how close to stand next to someone requires the ability to read and accurately interpret others' body language as well as understand the personal space boundaries of others. Thus, understanding personal space requires knowledge of nonverbal forms of communication, a topic well addressed in the literature (Howlin and Yates 1999; Ozonoff and Miller 1995; Williams 1989).

Introduce personal space

Group leaders should facilitate a discussion with group members regarding personal space, pointing out the importance of having a good understanding of personal space; it helps others feel comfortable around us. They should ensure that key aspects are covered such as:

- how close to stand to others keeping in mind our relationship with them (i.e., parents, teachers, peers, siblings, strangers, etc.)

- how we know when others are feeling uncomfortable (i.e., they back up, they try to end the conversation quickly, etc.)

- under what circumstances it is OK to touch others (i.e., hugging a family member, shaking hands when meeting someone, etc.).

Group leaders should discuss with group members how our personal space boundaries change depending on the person with whom we interact. For example, when interacting with parents, we sit and stand closer than we would if we were interacting with a teacher. Group leaders should highlight that we stand further away from people we do not know well and we stand closer to people we know very well. They should encourage group members to think about people they know and how close they think they should stand to those people based on their relationships with them. They should also facilitate a discussion regarding the difference between friends and acquaintances, as this will be important in the activity.

Personal Space Maps

Group leaders should explain to the group members that they will be making Personal Space Maps (see below). Group leaders should facilitate this activity and, depending on the number of group members, they may want to divide the group into smaller groups to make discussion easier.

Personal Space Maps

Materials

- Paper
- Markers or colored pencils
- Movie clips

Directions

Each group member should be given a piece of paper and should choose five colored pencils or markers. They should be instructed to write their name in the center of the paper and draw a small circle around their name. They should then draw four additional circles around their name, increasing in size and leaving space to write within each circle. The complete drawing should take up the majority of the paper.

Group members should then write the word "family" in the circle closest to their name, the word "friends" in the next outermost circle, the word "acquaintances" in the next outermost circle, and "strangers" in the outermost circle. Each of these words should be written in different colors and in a different color than the person's name. Thus, the picture should include five nested circles, resembling a "bull's eye."

Group leaders should explain that the Personal Space Map they are making will help them determine how close they should stand to others. They should also explain that those in the circle closest to their name, family, are people that they stand or sit closest to and that as the circles get further from their names, they should stand further away from those people. For example, they should sit or stand closer to friends than to strangers.

Group leaders should instruct the group members to look at the circle closest to their name, the one with the word "family" in it. The group members should use the same color marker or colored pencil that they used to write the word "family" to fill in the names of family members with whom they have close relationships. Examples include names of parents, siblings, or grandparents. Next, group leaders should instruct group members to choose the same color marker or colored pencil that they used to write the word "friends" and write the name of good friends in that circle. The same procedure should be followed for acquaintances. Obviously, no names should be written in the "stranger" circle.

After everyone has completed their Personal Space Maps, the group members should meet as a group to discuss the activity. Group leaders should pose questions such as, "What circle should teachers be in?" or "What circle should friends of your parents be in?" As the group discusses the answers, they can add to their Personal Space Maps. Group leaders should also have group members briefly practice in pairs the appropriate distance to stand from friends, acquaintances, and strangers, and facilitate this activity.

Snack and social time

During snack time, group members should be encouraged to pay special attention to how close they sit or stand to other group members and to watch for signals from others that they might be uncomfortable. If they sense that someone is uncomfortable, they should be encouraged to respond appropriately (i.e., backing up some). Again, group leaders should facilitate these social interactions.

Closing

At the end of the session, group members should be encouraged to appropriately tell each other goodbye and that they will see each other again next week. If there are any special upcoming occasions (e.g., birthdays, vacations, holidays), they should be encouraged to acknowledge them to one another. Distribute parent handouts to the parents and also provide parents with a copy of the teacher handout that they can share with their children's teachers.

Supplemental Session 5: Personal space

PARENT HANDOUT

What we did during group today

Today we talked about the importance of respecting the personal space boundaries of others. We talked about how we sit or stand closer to people we know well and that we sit or stand further away from people we do not know very well. We also talked about how we would know if we were standing too close to someone (e.g., the other person backs away, the other person tries to end the conversation quickly, etc.). We discussed when it is appropriate to touch others (e.g., hugging a family member, shaking hands when meeting someone). We also made our own Personal Space Maps to help us remember how close we should stand to others!

What to work on at home

At home, you can help your child practice good personal space boundaries with others. For example, you can look at your child's Personal Space Map and pretend to be one of the people on the map. Have your child determine how close he or she should stand to you, based on who you are pretending to be. Provide feedback, letting him or her know when he or she is standing too close or too far away.

Supplemental Session 5: Personal space

TEACHER HANDOUT

What we did in group this week

This week we talked about the importance of respecting the personal space boundaries of others. We talked about how we sit or stand closer to people we know well and that we sit or stand further away from people we do not know very well. We also talked about how we would know if we were standing too close to someone (e.g., the other person backs away, the other person tries to end the conversation quickly, etc.). We discussed when it is appropriate to touch others (e.g., hugging a family member, shaking hands when meeting someone). We also made our own Personal Space Maps to help us remember how close we should stand to others!

What to work on at school

At school, you can help the child practice good personal space boundaries with others. You can talk with the child about how close to stand to others at school—teachers, friends, other students in the class, students the child does not know well, the principal, parents, and so forth. You can even pretend to be some of these people and have the child stand the distance he or she thinks is appropriate, given who you are pretending to be. Provide feedback, letting him or her know when he or she is standing too close or too far away.

Supplemental Session 6: Friendship skills

Aim of session

The aim of this group session is to assist group members in identifying the qualities of a good friend and to learn skills to help them maintain friendships.

Empirical basis for the skill

The ability to maintain friendships is clearly related to possessing good conversational skills, emotion awareness, and the ability to understand and interpret nonverbal communication, topics heavily discussed in the literature (Cragar and Horvath 2003; Heitzman-Powell 2003; Howlin and Yates 1999; Marriage *et al.* 1995; Mesibov 1985; Ozonoff and Miller 1995; Williams 1989). In addition, Provencal (2003) specifically addresses the issue of initiating and maintaining relationships. Ozonoff and Miller (1995) include sharing, showing interest in others, and giving compliments, skills that are part of being a "good friend." A number of other studies also address skills related to friendship skills, such as discovering others' interests, teamwork, and cooperation (Cragar and Horvath 2003; Marriage *et al.* 1995; Provencal 2003; Williams 1989).

Introduce friendship skills

Group leaders should facilitate a discussion about friendship, posing questions such as:

- How do you make friends?

- What do friends do together?

- What should you talk about with friends?

- How do you maintain friendships?

- What makes someone a good or bad friend?

- How can you become a better friend?

Group leaders should ensure that the group discusses key issues. For example, with regard to making friends, they should ensure that the group discusses that we usually make friends with people who we see on a regular basis (i.e., at school, on a sports team, in girl/boy scouts, etc.), who have similar interests, and who like to talk with us. With regard to what friends do together, examples would include:

- talking

- playing games

- working on a project together

- going to do things together (i.e., to a movie, to the park, etc.)

- celebrating holidays or large events together.

With regard to what friends should talk about, group leaders should talk with the group about choosing appropriate chit-chat topics (see Session 6), focusing on topics about which *both* people are interested (i.e., common interests), and using how they know the person as a place to start. For example, if the group member knows the person from school, he or she could talk about topics related to school.

With regard to maintaining friendships, group leaders should highlight the importance of ongoing contact with the friend, such as continuing to do things with the friend, talking with the friend on the phone, and remembering and acknowledging important events in the friend's life (e.g., birthday, holidays the friend celebrates, and graduation or other accomplishments).

Group leaders should also facilitate a discussion regarding the characteristics that make someone a good or bad friend. "Good friend" examples include:

- honest
- friendly
- nice
- thoughtful
- warm

- common interests
- loyal
- helpful
- good listener
- trustworthy.

"Bad friend" examples include:

- dishonest
- mean
- degrading
- cold
- closed

- disinterested
- unavailable
- complaining
- self-centered.

Group leaders should then help group members discuss how they can become better friends, possessing more of the "good friend" traits and characteristics. For example, a group member who tends to forget his or her friends' birthdays could work on remembering these birthdays (i.e., writing them on the calendar) and making birthday cards for those friends. If a group member tends to talk too much and not listen enough, he or she could work on talking less and listening more. Each group member should identify at least one way they can become a better friend, and a group leader should write down on separate index cards the group members' names and their "friendship goals."

"Friendship Card game"

Group leaders should introduce the Friendship Card game (see below).

"Friendship Card" game

Materials

- Index cards
- Markers

Directions

Prior to the start of group, group leaders should prepare decks of cards with characteristics of a "good friend." The decks can be created by writing a positive characteristic on each index card. All decks of cards should be identical; they should have the same characteristics on them. The following are examples of positive traits that can be put on the cards:

- fun
- loyal
- cool
- common interests
- trustworthy
- honest
- nice
- friendly
- talkative
- shares
- open
- good listener
- warm
- nonjudgmental
- helpful
- thoughtful.

Each group member should receive a deck of cards and should be instructed to select three cards that represent the traits they think are most important when looking for a friend. If the group is small, the discussion of the cards can be done as a group. If the group is large, the group members can be divided into smaller groups. Each group member should then share with the group (or their smaller group) the reason they chose those cards and examples of how a friend would demonstrate that trait. For example, if the trait chosen was "helpful," the group member should talk about why that trait is important to them and then provide an example of a friend being helpful (e.g., helping find something that was lost).

Next, group members should put all the cards back in the deck and then choose three cards that represent traits they think they possess as a friend. Again, the discussion of these cards can be done as a group or can be done in smaller groups. Each group member should share with the group (or with their smaller group) how they think they possess those particular traits, providing examples of how they would demonstrate that trait within a friendship.

Following the Friendship Card game, group leaders should distribute each group member's index card with his or her new "friendship goal" that was discussed earlier in the group. Group leaders should assist group members in thinking of ways they can work on their particular goals.

Snack and social time

During snack time, group members should be encouraged to work on being a "good friend," demonstrating the traits of a "good friend." If applicable, group members can also work on their individual friendship goals. Again, group leaders should facilitate these social interactions.

Closing

At the end of the session, group members should be encouraged to appropriately tell each other goodbye and that they will see each other again next week. If there are any special upcoming occasions (e.g., birthdays, vacations, holidays), they should be encouraged to acknowledge them to one another, and group leaders should point out that this is a "good friend" trait. Distribute parent handouts to the parents and also provide parents with a copy of the teacher handout that they can share with their children's teachers. Group leaders should ensure that group members share their "friendship goal" index cards with their parents in order to facilitate the parents encouraging their children to work on these goals.

Supplemental Session 6: Friendship skills

PARENT HANDOUT

What we did during group today

Today we talked about friendship, including how to make friends, what friends do together, what friends talk about with one another, how to maintain friendships, what makes someone a "good" or "bad" friend, and how to become a better friend. We played the Friendship Card game in which we selected cards that represented the traits we think are important in a friend. We also selected cards that represented characteristics we think we possess within friendships. We talked about why we selected those cards and provided examples of how those "good friend" characteristics could be demonstrated in a friendship. We also set goals for ourselves regarding how we can become a better friend (your child should have an index card with his or her goal on it).

What to work on at home

At home, you can talk with your child about what makes someone a good friend. Tell your child the qualities you like in him or her and have your child identify the characteristics he or she likes in you. Ask your child to talk with you about what makes someone a good friend and encourage him or her to work on the "friendship goal" he/she set in group today. When you see your child demonstrating good friendship skills, positively reinforce him or her, stating specifically what you saw and liked.

Supplemental Session 6: Friendship skills

TEACHER HANDOUT

What we did in group this week

This week we talked about friendship, including how to make friends, what friends do together, what friends talk about with one another, how to maintain friendships, what makes someone a "good" or "bad" friend, and how to become a better friend. We played the Friendship Card game in which we selected cards that represented the traits we think are important in a friend. We also selected cards that represented characteristics we think we possess within friendships. We talked about why we selected those cards and provided examples of how those "good friend" characteristics could be demonstrated in a friendship. We also set goals for ourselves regarding how we can become a better friend.

What to work on at school

At school, you can remind the child to use good friendship skills when interacting with other students. You can also encourage the child to make more friends at school by talking about how to try and make friends and providing him or her with feedback about his or her plan. Then, you can facilitate the child following the plan you developed together. You can even set the child up for a successful interaction by encouraging him or her to start interacting more frequently with a child who has similar interests.

Supplemental Session 7: Perspective-taking and empathy

Aim of session

The aim of this group session is to help group members show appropriate empathy toward others and increase their ability to take the perspective of others.

Empirical basis for the skill

The ability to take the perspective of others is directly related to the ability to show empathy for others. Perspective-taking skills tend to be an area of difficulty among individuals with AS and can negatively impact social relationships, a topic well discussed in the literature (Cragar and Horvath 2003; Marriage *et al.* 1995; Ozonoff and Miller 1995; Provencal 2003; Whitaker *et al.* 1998). It is important to address the ability to take the perspective of others and to show appropriate empathy toward others.

Introduce perspective-taking

Group leaders should facilitate a discussion highlighting that people can have different perspectives in various situations. They should point out that people can have different physical perspectives and people can have different opinions or perspectives, and should ask group members to share examples of each of these issues. For example, depending upon where two people may be standing, they may have two different physical perspectives, where one person can see something the other person cannot. Also, people may have different opinions or perspectives about a movie, a book, a game played at recess, and so forth.

Next, group leaders should lead a discussion regarding how we can guess how other people feel about a situation based on how most people feel in that situation. They should pose various scenarios and have the group members guess how most people would feel in that situation, highlighting that the process of guessing how other people feel based on their given situation is a form of perspective-taking. Examples include:

- when a relative dies (sad)
- when getting ready for a big trip (excited/happy)
- doing poorly on a test (upset/sad)
- being made fun of (mad/sad)
- getting a good grade on an assignment (happy).

Perspective-taking roleplays

Group leaders should divide the group members into pairs. In these pairs, group members should roleplay a situation in which they each have a different opinion or perspective about a movie or a book. Then, group leaders should mix up the pairs and have each pair engage in another roleplay. In this second roleplay, one group member should be given a scenario such as the ones discussed above and the other person in the pair should guess how the first group member would feel in that situation. If the two group members feel differently about the situation, a group leader should help them discuss why they feel differently.

Introduce empathy

Group leaders should facilitate a discussion regarding empathy. They should highlight that being empathetic is important in making and keeping friends because being empathetic communicates to others that you care about them. Group leaders should ask group members to think about how perspective-taking and empathy are related. They should point out that in order to be empathetic, you need to be able to make a good guess about how the other person is feeling, based upon the given situation.

Group leaders should remind group members that they have already talked about how to respond to someone who has shared emotional news (see Session 8) and point out that in this group they will focus on conveying empathy to the other person. If necessary, group leaders should review some appropriate verbal responses to the situations discussed in Session 8. They should then ask group members how they think they can convey empathy to the other person. For example, you should identify the emotion the other person is probably feeling, make an appropriate statement in response to the given situation (see Session 8), focus on the other person and what he or she is saying, repeat or rephrase what the other person says or feels to communicate understanding, use an appropriate tone of voice and facial expression, and offer to help in some way, if applicable. Group leaders should also point out that making a brief empathetic statement and then moving on to another topic is not being empathetic.

Empathy roleplays

If group members seem to be having a difficult time grasping the idea of being empathetic to others, group leaders can roleplay good empathetic responses and responses that are not empathetic, asking group members how to "fix" the no-empathy roleplay. Group leaders should divide group members into pairs for the roleplays. Each pair will perform a roleplay in front of the group and the group members will guess whether the pair is roleplaying an appropriate empathetic response or a no-empathy response. If the pair has performed a no-empathy response, group members should discuss how to "fix" the roleplay. If the pair has performed an empathetic response, group members should discuss how the group member conveyed empathy to the other person. Each pair should perform two roleplays, switching parts so that each group member has the opportunity to respond to a situation.

Empathy roleplay scenarios

1. You just found out that a family member has become very sick.
2. You got a new puppy!
3. Your parents told you that your family will not be able to go on vacation this summer.
4. You tried out for a sports team and made it!
5. You just had an argument with your parent.
6. One of your favorite toys was stolen at school today.
7. One of your friends said something mean to you.
8. You dropped your lunch tray at school and everyone stared and laughed at you.

Snack and social time

During snack time, group members should be encouraged to be empathetic to others as they share what is going on in their lives. They can also work on taking the emotional perspective of others and check in with others about their accuracy. Of course, group leaders should facilitate these interactions.

Closing

At the end of the session, group members should be encouraged to appropriately tell each other goodbye and that they will see each other again next week. If there are any special upcoming occasions (e.g., birthdays, vacations, holidays), they should be encouraged to acknowledge them to one another. In addition, if someone has had a rough week, has made an accomplishment, or has something stressful coming up in the next week, group members should be encouraged to respond empathetically with assistance from group leaders, as necessary. Distribute parent handouts to the parents and also provide parents with a copy of the teacher handout that they can share with their children's teachers.

Supplemental Session 7: Perspective-taking and empathy

PARENT HANDOUT

What we did during group today

Today we talked about the importance of being able to take the perspective of others, especially the emotional perspective of others. We discussed how perspective-taking is related to being able to show empathy toward others. We talked about demonstrating empathy by:

- identifying the feeling of the other person
- focusing on what the other person is saying
- reflecting back to the person what they said to communicate understanding
- using appropriate facial expressions and tone of voice to match the situation.

We practiced these skills by roleplaying with other group members and identifying how the group members showed empathy.

What to work on at home

At home, you can help your child accurately identify the feelings of others. One fun way to do this is to discreetly "people watch" and ask your child to guess the emotions of others based on the nonverbal cues he or she can see. You can also encourage your child to think of others and how they might feel in certain situations. For example, if you see a stray object in a parking lot or along the street with your child, you can ask him or her how the person who lost that object might feel. Praise your child when he or she demonstrates empathy and be specific about what you saw and what you liked. For example, you could say, "I really like how you shared your pretzels with Susie after hers fell on the floor."

Supplemental Session 7: Perspective-taking and empathy

TEACHER HANDOUT

What we did in group this week

This week we talked about the importance of being able to take the perspective of others, especially the emotional perspective of others. We discussed how perspective-taking is related to being able to show empathy toward others. We talked about demonstrating empathy by:

- identifying the feeling of the other person
- focusing on what the other person is saying
- reflecting back to the person what they said to communicate understanding
- using appropriate facial expressions and tone of voice to match the situation.

We practiced these skills by roleplaying with other group members and identifying how the group members showed empathy.

What to work on at school

At school, you can ask the child how others must feel when an opportune situation arises. For example, if you are walking by the lost and found box at school, you can ask him or her how the people who lost those items must feel. If you are walking by the nurse's office and another student is with the nurse, you can ask him or her to guess how that student is feeling. If you are walking by a bulletin board with outstanding work displayed, you can ask him or her how those students might feel about having their work displayed. Also, praise the child when he or she demonstrates empathy and be specific about what you saw and what you liked. For example, you could say, "I really like how you offered to help Kate pick up her papers after she dropped her folder."

Supplemental Session 8: Flexibility and adaptability

Aim of session

The aim of this group session is to help group members increase their ability to cope with changes that occur in their lives—to help them become more flexible and adaptable.

Empirical basis for the skill

Individuals with AS often have difficulty adapting to change and being flexible. In fact, lack of flexibility and adaptability is part of the diagnostic criteria of AS in the *DSM-IV-TR* (APA 2000). Even historically, preservation of sameness, the desire for everything to follow an orderly and predictable routine, was outlined by Kanner as diagnostic criteria for what he called early infantile autism and what is now thought of as AS (Wing 1991). Despite the fact that difficulties with flexibility and adaptability are often present in individuals with AS, few studies in the current literature apart from Williams (1989) have specifically addressed these issues. A few studies (Attwood 2003; Howlin and Yates 1999) discuss related issues such as stress and anxiety, which may result from difficulty adapting to change.

Introduce flexibility

Group leaders should discuss with the group that being flexible and adaptable is an important life skill because changes are inevitable in life. They should also highlight that being able to effectively cope with changes, expected or unexpected, will help them function more successfully in life and in social relationships. Group leaders should facilitate a discussion about flexibility and adaptability. They should pose questions such as:

- What does it mean to be flexible or adaptable?

- What should you do when things don't go the way you had planned?

- How should you respond to changes?

Group leaders should ensure that the group discusses that changes always occur in life and that many are essentially unavoidable and out of our control. They should discuss with the group how to appropriately respond to changes in life. For example, they should introduce the concept of self-talk, a coping strategy in which group members make positive statements to themselves. Examples include:

- "I can handle this, no problem."

- "Change happens and it is OK."

- "I know how to be flexible."

Group leaders should also discuss relaxation techniques that group members can utilize to reduce anxiety about changes. Examples would include taking three deep breaths, counting to ten, stretching, and so forth. Self-talk and relaxation techniques can be combined.

Group leaders should also ask group members to think of what they should say to someone who tells them about a change. For example, if a teacher tells them that the day's schedule will be different due to an assembly, they should say something such as, "OK, no problem."

Introduce adaptability roleplays

Group leaders should introduce the roleplay activity to the group members. They should tell the group members that they will have the opportunity to respond to a number of situations that involve change and they should respond both verbally and nonverbally, making a statement and using self-talk and/or relaxation techniques.

Group leaders should explain to group members that they will be lining up and doing "speed roleplays" in which the person at the front of the line will respond to the given situation and then will go to the end of the line, allowing the next person in line to respond to a situation. If a group member gets "stuck," other group members and, of course, group leaders can intervene and provide suggestions.

"Speed" adaptability roleplay scenarios

1. You were looking forward to going to art today but your teacher tells you that due to an assembly the class will not be going to art today.

2. You have an after-school practice today and the principal just said over the loud speaker that all after-school meetings are canceled for today due to bad weather.

3. This morning your parent told you that the family is going out to dinner tonight at your favorite restaurant. After school, your parent tells you that the family won't be going out to eat because another family member is sick.

4. Your class usually meets in one room but today your teacher announces that the class must move to a different room.

5. Your class is scheduled to go on a field trip later in the week and the principal tells the class that the field trip is canceled due to a lack of adult chaperones.

6. You love to play video games and when you get home from school your hand control does not work.

7. You are looking forward to watching a TV program on cable and when you turn on the TV to watch it, the cable is out and you will not be able to watch the program.

8. You were invited to a birthday party and you want to sit by your friend, but when you get to the table there are no spots left next to your friend.

9. You want to play outside after school but when you get home your parent tells you that you first must clean your room.

10. You usually sit in a certain spot in music class but when you walk into the room, someone is already sitting in your usual spot.

Snack and social time

During snack time, group members should be encouraged to be flexible and adaptable. For example, if a group member wants a particular type of snack and none of that kind is left, he or she should strive to be flexible about his or her snack choice. Also, if they usually sit in the same seats each session, encourage them to try sitting in another seat. In fact, in the next group session, group leaders could change the snack time and have it at the beginning of group instead of at the end, or switch the room in which the group will meet and assist group members in being flexible and adaptable.

Closing

At the end of the session, group members should be encouraged to appropriately tell each other goodbye and that they will see each other again next week. If there are any special upcoming occasions (e.g., birthdays, vacations, holidays), they should be encouraged to acknowledge them to one another. Distribute parent handouts to the parents and also provide parents with a copy of the teacher handout that they can share with their children's teachers.

Supplemental Session 8: Flexibility and adaptability

PARENT HANDOUT

What we did during group today

Today we talked about the importance of being flexible and adaptable when changes occur in life. We discussed that changes always happen in life and that many times the changes are not within our control. We talked about how we can remain calm when unexpected changes occur. We can make positive self-statements such as, "I can handle this" or "Change happens and it is OK." We also talked about trying to relax by taking deep breaths or counting to ten. We practiced these skills in a round of "speed" roleplays in which scenarios were presented to us and we had to respond appropriately.

What to work on at home

At home, you can encourage your child to be flexible and adaptable when changes occur. Remind your child to use the relaxation and self-talk skills he or she learned in group. You can model for your child appropriate responses to changes in life by making him or her aware of how you are being flexible. For example, if you are planning to stop by the store but, due to traffic, stopping would make you late for a meeting, you can tell your child that you are being flexible by planning to stop by the store after the meeting instead. Reinforce your child for being flexible and when you must tell him or her about a change, remind him or her to be flexible!

Supplemental Session 8: Flexibility and adaptability

TEACHER HANDOUT

What we did in group this week

This week we talked about the importance of being flexible and adaptable when changes occur in life. We discussed that changes always happen in life and that many times the changes are not within our control. We talked about how we can remain calm when unexpected changes occur. We can make positive self-statements such as, "I can handle this" or "Change happens and it is OK." We also talked about trying to relax by taking deep breaths or counting to ten. We practiced these skills in a round of "speed" roleplays in which scenarios were presented to us and we had to respond appropriately.

What to work on at school

At school, you can encourage the child to be flexible and adaptable when changes occur. Remind the child to use the relaxation and self-talk skills he or she learned in group. Reinforce the child when he or she is flexible. For example, if the day's schedule changes and the child responds well, you could say "I really like how you stayed calm and said 'OK, no problem' when I told you that our class schedule was going to be different today." When you are about to announce a change, you can encourage the child to be flexible and adaptable.

Supplemental Session 9: Politeness

Aim of session

The aim of this group session is to help group members recognize when they may come across as being rude and inadvertently hurt others' feelings. This group session aims to help group members learn how to be honest and still be polite.

Empirical basis for the skill

Although being polite is not commonly referred to in the literature, being polite and not hurting others' feelings is essential in establishing and maintaining friendships, a topic emphasized by Provencal (2003). Politeness is also related to perspective-taking skills; in order to be polite and avoid hurting others' feelings, one must be able to take the emotional perspective of the other person. Perspective-taking skills are well discussed in the literature (Cragar and Horvath 2003; Marriage *et al.* 1995; Ozonoff and Miller 1995; Provencal 2003; Whitaker *et al.* 1998). Barnhill and colleagues (2002) discussed that individuals with AS have sometimes been described as being rude, tactless, hurtful or insensitive due to their social skills difficulties. Williams (1989) specifically addressed the topic of individuals with AS coming across as being rude.

Introduce politeness

Group leaders should talk with the group members about the importance of being polite and not hurting others' feelings, pointing out that this skill is important in establishing and maintaining friendships. They should then facilitate a discussion about what being polite means. Examples include having good manners (e.g., saying please and thank you), offering to help others when they need help, complimenting others, and so forth.

Group leaders should discuss with group members how to tell the truth without hurting others' feelings, ensuring the group members discuss that people can have different opinions about things and that, even if you disagree with someone, you can find a way to talk with that person without hurting their feelings. They should point out that group members should strive to find the "nice thing" about something and use that to respond. This skill is important in not coming across as rude to others. For example, if you receive a gift you do not like, you can simply say, "Thank you for the gift." Another example would be if you disagree with someone else's opinion. For example, you and a friend may have different opinions about a movie; your friend may have liked the movie and you may have not liked it. You can politely disagree with your friend by something such as, "I'm really glad we saw the movie together, but I actually did not like it as much as you did. I liked parts of it, though; what was your favorite part?"

Introduce "What Should You Say?" game

Group leaders should introduce the "What Should You Say?" game (see below), explaining to the group members that they will be presented with scenarios and will need to think of the polite (non-rude) way to respond. Group leaders should divide the group members into pairs in order to practice responding to the scenarios. Each member of the pair should have the opportunity to be the "responder" in at least one scenario. Of course, group leaders should be available to facilitate these roleplays.

What Should You Say? game

Scenarios

1. A classmate gets a new haircut that you do not like. He or she asks you what you think of the haircut.

2. Your class all read the same book and you really liked the book but your friend did not. Your friend says he or she hated the book and then asks you what you think of the book.

3. Your sibling is really excited about making the soccer team but you don't like soccer. Your sibling comes home and tells you how excited he or she is about making the team.

4. Your friend had a singing part in a school musical performance and you think he or she performed poorly. Your friend comes up to you after the performance and asks you what you thought of his or her solo.

5. You and your friend like to watch the same TV show. You did not like last night's episode of the show. Your friend calls and tells you he or she really liked the episode and then asks you what you thought of the episode.

Introduce "Goofy Gift Exchange" game

If time permits, group leaders can introduce the "Goofy Gift Exchange" game (see below). They should explain to group members that they will be receiving a gift and will need to respond appropriately, in a way that will not hurt the gift giver's feelings.

"Goofy Gift Exchange" game

Materials

- Gag gifts (e.g., paperclips, index cards, a piece of wood, etc.)
- Wrapping paper
- Tape

Directions

Prior to the start of group, group leaders should collect gag gifts and wrap them. Each group member should have one gift. Group members should sit in a circle and open their gifts one at a time and respond appropriately. They are to pretend that they received this gift from a family member who is present in the room. As each group member opens his or her gift, the other group members can provide suggestions, as needed.

Snack and social time

During snack time, group members should be encouraged to chit-chat with one another, paying special attention to being polite and not hurting other group members' feelings.

Closing

At the end of the session, group members should be encouraged to appropriately tell each other goodbye and that they will see each other again next week. If there are any special upcoming occasions (e.g., birthdays, vacations, holidays), they should be encouraged to acknowledge them to one another. Distribute parent handouts to the parents and also provide parents with a copy of the teacher handout that they can share with their children's teachers.

Supplemental Session 9: Politeness

PARENT HANDOUT

What we did during group today

Today we talked about the importance of being polite and striving to not hurt others' feelings. We talked about how to look for the "nice thing" about something and then using that to respond to the other person, so that we do not hurt the other person's feelings. In addition, we learned how to disagree politely. We then practiced responding politely to various situations from disagreeing with a friend to receiving a gift we do not like.

What to work on at home

At home, you can help your child continue to learn to look for the "nice things" about situations and then to use that to respond to the other person. You can use real-life teaching opportunities and roleplay some situations with your child. You can also talk with your child about times you have had to be sure to respond to someone in a way that would not hurt the other person's feelings.

Supplemental Session 9: Politeness

TEACHER HANDOUT

What we did in group this week

This week we talked about the importance of being polite and striving to not hurt others' feelings. We talked about how to look for the "nice thing" about something and then using that to respond to the other person, so that we do not hurt the other person's feelings. In addition, we learned how to disagree politely. We then practiced responding politely to various situations from disagreeing with a friend to receiving a gift we do not like.

What to work on at school

At school, you can encourage the child to identify the "nice thing" about a situation and then to use that to help him or her respond to someone else, paying special attention to not hurting the other person's feelings. You can practice roleplaying various situations with the child and assist him or her in determining an appropriate and polite response. You can also talk with the child about times you have had to be sure to respond to someone in a way that would not hurt the other person's feelings.

Supplemental Session 10: Understanding sarcasm and figures of speech

Aim of session

The aim of this group session is to increase group members' understanding of sarcasm and figures of speech.

Empirical basis for the skill

Individuals with AS often have difficulty understanding sarcasm and figures of speech, and more broadly, difficulty appreciating humor. Weiss and Harris (2001) discuss how individuals with AS often demonstrate notable difficulty appreciating humor. In addition, Mesibov (1985) specifically addresses the topic of appreciating humor in his group intervention.

Introduce sarcasm

Group leaders should facilitate a discussion with group members regarding what being sarcastic means, how to tell if someone is being sarcastic, and sarcasm's role in humor. They should be sure to point out that being sarcastic is a way of being funny and teasing others. They should also talk with group members about how they will know if someone has taken the sarcastic teasing too far, to the point of being attacking.

Group leaders should ensure that the group discusses the important role of tone of voice in telling if someone is being sarcastic, and illustrate this with examples. They should also talk with group members about how many sarcastic statements, if taken literally, would be compliments. However, when someone is being sarcastic, he or she actually means the opposite of what they are saying. For example, if you are running a race and come in last and someone says, "Wow, you run like a cheetah!" they are really teasing you about coming in last in the race. It is the tone of voice (and sometimes facial expression) that tells you if the person is being sarcastic or complimentary.

Introduce figures of speech

Group leaders should facilitate a discussion with group members regarding the use of figures of speech, and explain that there are common phrases (figures of speech) people say that if interpreted literally would mean something completely different than what the person actually means. They should ask group members to try and think of examples, and group leaders can provide examples as well. They should also be sure to talk with group members about using contextual cues to figure out what the person means. In addition, group members should be encouraged to check in with an adult, such as a parent or teacher, when they are unsure about the meaning of a phrase.

Introduce "Sarcasm and Figures of Speech Jeopardy" game

Group leaders should introduce "Sarcasm and Figures of Speech Jeopardy" to group members (see below).

"Sarcasm and Figures of Speech Jeopardy" game

Materials

- Cards with the questions written on them
- Piece of paper or chalkboard to keep score
- Bells or other noisemaking devices for participants to "ring in" to give their answer
- Small prize

Directions

Group leaders should make two categories of cards with questions written on them prior to the start of group. One category should be "sarcasm," in which statements are written on the cards and group leaders will read the statement using either a sarcastic tone of voice or a complimentary tone of voice. The tone of voice to be used should be indicated on the card. The other category should be "figures of speech" in which common phrases are written on the cards. See below for card ideas. For the "sarcasm" category, the group members must guess whether the group leader is being sarcastic or complimentary. For the "figures of speech" category, the group members must explain what the common phrase really means (*not* its literal meaning).

Depending upon the size of the group, group members may participate as individuals or group leaders may wish to divide the members into pairs or teams. Each team or individual should have a signaling device in order to "ring in" to give their answers. One group member or team should be chosen to select a category first. That group member has the opportunity to answer the question first (about 5–10 seconds) before the rest of the group may "ring in" to answer. Group members must provide the correct answer and provide an explanation of how they arrived at that answer to the group. Whoever answers the question correctly gets to choose the next category.

If no individual or team can provide the correct answer, group leaders should facilitate a discussion to arrive at the correct answer. The team or individual with the most points at the end of the game wins a small prize.

Card ideas for "Sarcasm and Figures of Speech Jeopardy" game

Sarcasm

1. You keep answering questions incorrectly in class. A classmate says to you, "Well, aren't you an Einstein today?!" [sarcastic]

2. You just won an award at school. Someone comes up to you and says, "Congratulations on your award. You should be proud of yourself!" [complimentary]

3. You are a really quiet person and someone tells you, "You need to settle down and not be so loud!" [sarcastic]

4. You are a very slow runner in P.E. Someone comes up to you and says, "You're really fast!" [sarcastic]

5. You are a fast runner in P.E. Someone comes up to you and says, "Wow! You're a really fast runner!" [complimentary]

6. After a soccer game in which you made five goals, someone comes up to you and says, "You are really good at playing soccer." [complimentary]

7. You did not do very well while playing in a basketball game. In fact, you kept missing the baskets. Someone comes up to you and says, "Well aren't you a regular Michael Jordan?!" [sarcastic]

8. You tell a joke and everyone laughs. Someone comes up to you and says, "You are really funny! Where did you hear that joke?" [complimentary]

9. You tell a joke and no one laughs. Someone says, "Well that went over well…where did you hear that joke?!" [sarcastic]

10. Someone comes up to you at school and says, "I really like the shirt you have on today." [complimentary]

Figures of Speech

1. You're out in left field.

2. Chill out.

3. What's up?

4. You missed the boat!

5. You are getting carried away!

6. You are treading on thin ice.

7. Get back on track.

8. Don't put all of your eggs in one basket.

9. Do you have the time?

10. Get your head on straight.

One potential problem that may arise when playing "Sarcasm and Figures of Speech Jeopardy" is that group members may become upset if they or their team are not winning. It is important that group leaders facilitate the game. To encourage group members to be good sports, group leaders can hand out small stickers, sweets, or other little prizes to group members who are being good sports. In fact, being a good sport is a skill that can help individuals with AS have more positive experiences with peers, especially at recess or other times when competitive games are generally played. Being a good sport is the topic of Supplemental Session 4.

Snack and social time

During snack time, group members should be encouraged to chit-chat with one another, paying special attention to any figures of speech or sarcasm other group members or group leaders use. In fact, group leaders can purposely use sarcasm and figures of speech and ask the group members what they think the group leader means. Group members should be encouraged to help one another figure out what the group leader means.

Closing

At the end of the session, group members should be encouraged to appropriately tell each other goodbye and that they will see each other again next week. If there are any special upcoming occasions (e.g., birthdays, vacations, holidays), they should be encouraged to acknowledge them to one another. Distribute parent handouts to the parents and also provide parents with a copy of the teacher handout that they can share with their children's teachers.

Supplemental Session 10: Understanding sarcasm and figures of speech

PARENT HANDOUT

What we did during group today

Today we talked about sarcasm and figures of speech. We discussed what being sarcastic means, how to tell if someone is being sarcastic, the importance of listening to the person's tone of voice in order to tell if they are being sarcastic, and sarcasm's role in humor. We talked about how if we accidentally interpreted someone's sarcastic statement literally, we might think we were getting a compliment instead of being teased. We also discussed that there are common phrases that people say that should not be interpreted literally (e.g., "you missed the boat"). We practiced interpreting common phrases and determining if someone is being sarcastic or complimentary in a game of "Sarcasm and Figures of Speech Jeopardy"

What to work on at home

At home, you can help your child by pointing out examples of sarcasm and figures of speech. Tell him or her what common phrases actually mean. There are many common phrases that individuals use that are not meant to be interpreted literally, and you can help your child learn the correct meaning of these phrases by pointing them out when others use them and by using them yourself. Be sure to check in with your child to ensure he or she has correctly interpreted the phrase.

Supplemental Session 10: Understanding sarcasm and figures of speech

TEACHER HANDOUT

What we did in group this week

This week we talked about sarcasm and figures of speech. We discussed what being sarcastic means, how to tell if someone is being sarcastic, the importance of listening to the person's tone of voice in order to tell if they are being sarcastic, and sarcasm's role in humor. We talked about how if we accidentally interpreted someone's sarcastic statement literally, we might think we were getting a compliment instead of being teased. We also discussed that there are common phrases that people say that should not be interpreted literally (e.g., "you missed the boat"). We practiced interpreting common phrases and determining if someone is being sarcastic or complimentary in a game of "Sarcasm and Figures of Speech Jeopardy"

What to work on at school

At school, you can help the child by pointing out examples of sarcasm and figures of speech as they come up in the school setting. Be sure to check in with the child about the interpretation of common phrases and provide correction as needed. There are many common phrases that individuals use that are not meant to be interpreted literally, and you can help the child learn about these phrases by pointing out when others use them and by using them yourself. You can also help the child recognize sarcasm by using "real-life" examples as teaching moments.

Adolescent Supplemental Session 1: Hanging out

Aim of session

The aim of this group session is to teach adolescent group members about how to "hang out" with friends and acquaintances.

Empirical basis for the skill

The ability to hang out with friends is a basic friendship skill of adolescence. They are moving from playing together to "hanging out" together. Hanging out can be a difficult skill for individuals with AS because it is usually not highly activity-based and relies heavily on conversational skills, generally a difficult skill for adolescents with AS. A number of basic component skills working together make up the ability to hang out successfully with peers, including initiating and maintaining conversations (Cragar and Horvath 2003; Heitzman-Powell 2003; Howlin and Yates 1999; Marriage *et al.* 1995; Ozonoff and Miller 1995; Williams 1989), accurately interpreting and displaying nonverbal behavior (Barnhill *et al.* 2002; Howlin and Yates 1999; Ozonoff and Miller 1995; Williams 1989), and appreciating humor (Mesibov 1985; Weiss and Harris 2001).

Introduce hanging out skills

Group leaders should facilitate a discussion with group members regarding what hanging out means, what you should do when hanging out with others, what to talk about when hanging out with others, what people usually do while they are hanging out, what makes someone a good person to hang out with, and so forth. They should highlight the importance of good conversational skills (especially chit-chatting) and review those skills as necessary (see Sessions 6, 7, and 8). Group leaders should ask group members to think of good conversational, chit-chat topics. Examples include:

- current movies
- popular adolescent TV shows
- school events
- sports.

They should point out that it is important to stick with the topic people are already talking about or to choose a topic directly related to what they are already talking about.

Group leaders should also facilitate a discussion with group members regarding the social skill of "blending in" when hanging out in a group. They can discuss with group members how important it becomes in adolescence to "fit in" to social groups and to "blend in" with your peers. Group leaders should highlight that this does *not* mean that group members should go along with what others tell them to do, especially things they know are wrong. They should point out that blending in socially means following others' lead on conversational topics. They can also discuss with group members that they can find a peer who has good social skills as a model to help them be successful in their own social interactions. For example, if both are at a party, the adolescent with AS can use the adolescent with good social skills as a model of how to hang out—what to talk about, how to sit, when to laugh, and so on.

Group leaders should talk with group members about the relaxed nature of hanging out. When people are hanging out, they are usually sitting or standing in relaxed ways and it is usually a time of casual conversation. Group leaders can also point out that it is also a time when adolescents like to be funny, usually by telling jokes, sharing funny stories, or teasing other peers. In fact, it may be helpful for adolescents to have already covered Understanding sarcasm and figures of speech (see Supplemental Session 10) because these issues are pertinent in knowing how to interpret what others are saying and knowing when it is appropriate to laugh while hanging out with peers.

Hanging out party

Teaching group members how to hang out with peers can be rather abstract. In order to make the skills more concrete, group leaders should set up a "hanging out party" within the group session. This time will involve having music playing in the background, arranging the room's furniture to simulate someone's home, and having "finger foods" available for the group members to snack on. Group leaders should explain to group members that they will be practicing their hanging out skills during this activity. (This activity will obviously include the snack and social time of group.)

Group leaders should participate in this activity and should provide prompts to group members as necessary. They should essentially "coach" group members during this activity by "whispering in the ear," discreetly providing coaching to group members in order to facilitate positive social interactions. Group leaders can prompt group members regarding topics of conversation, when to laugh, how to sit, how to initiate an interaction with someone, staying on topic, and so forth.

Closing

At the end of the session, group members should be encouraged to appropriately tell each other goodbye and that they will see each other again next week. If there are any special upcoming occasions (e.g., birthdays, vacations, holidays), they should be encouraged to acknowledge them to one another. Distribute parent handouts to the parents and also provide parents with a copy of the teacher handout that they can share with their adolescent's teachers.

Adolescent Supplemental Session 1: Hanging out

PARENT HANDOUT

What we did during group today

Today we talked about how to hang out with our adolescent peers. We discussed what hanging out means, what you should do when hanging out with others, what to talk about when hanging out with others, what people usually do while they are hanging out, what makes someone a good person to hang out with, and "blending in" socially. We had the opportunity to practice our hanging out skills in group today by having a party. Our group leaders provided us with coaching during this party so that we could practice demonstrating good social skills.

What to work on at home

At home, you can encourage your adolescent to brainstorm with you good, "safe" topics to discuss when hanging out with peers. You can also ask your adolescent what he or she should do if unsure of what to do when hanging out with others. You can help your adolescent remember to look for a good social skills peer model and to use that person to help him or her figure out what to do in social settings with peers. In fact, you can help your adolescent determine who he or she knows that would be a good social skills model.

Adolescent Supplemental Session 1: Hanging out

TEACHER HANDOUT

What we did in group this week

This week we talked about how to hang out with our adolescent peers. We discussed what hanging out means, what you should do when hanging out with others, what to talk about when hanging out with others, what people usually do while they are hanging out, what makes someone a good person to hang out with, and "blending in" socially. We had the opportunity to practice our hanging out skills in group today by having a party. Our group leaders provided us with coaching during this party so that we could practice demonstrating good social skills.

What to work on at school

At school, you can encourage the adolescent to work on his or her hanging out skills during appropriate times at school, such as before and after school and during lunch. In fact, you can even provide some coaching for the adolescent, providing suggestions to him or her that will foster successful peer interactions. You can brainstorm with the adolescent good, "safe" topics of chit-chat when hanging out with peers. You can also help the adolescent choose a good social skills peer model and remind the adolescent to use that person to help him or her figure out what to do in social situations with peers.

Adolescent Supplemental Session 2: School dances

Aim of session

The aim of this group session is to teach group members about appropriate social behavior at school dances.

Empirical basis for the skill

In adolescence, a number of new social occasions arise, including school dances. A school dance is a highly social event, requiring a combination of a number of good social skills including conversational skills (Cragar and Horvath 2003; Heitzman-Powell 2003; Howlin and Yates 1999; Marriage *et al.* 1995; Ozonoff and Miller 1995; Williams 1989), accurately interpreting and displaying nonverbal behavior (Barnhill *et al.* 2002; Howlin and Yates 1999; Ozonoff and Miller 1995; Williams 1989), appreciating humor (Mesibov 1985; Weiss and Harris 2001), and hanging out with friends.

Introduce school dances

Group leaders should discuss with group members the topic of school dances, being sure to discuss issues such as appropriate dress, what they think occurs at a dance, what people do at a dance, how to ask someone to dance, and so forth. They can encourage group members who have been to a school dance to share their experiences with the group. Group leaders should ask the group members what social skills they would need to demonstrate when attending a school dance (i.e., good conversational skills, hanging out skills, accurately interpreting and displaying nonverbal behavior, etc.).

Group leaders should talk with group members in more detail about what people do at a dance. Adolescents talk, hang out, joke around, eat/drink refreshments, and dance when they attend a school dance. It is a good idea to have already covered hanging out skills (see Adolescent Supplemental Session 1) prior to the current session, as adolescents "hang out" together when they attend a school dance. Group leaders should remind group members of the hanging out skills learned in a previous group session. It would also be helpful if group members had already covered understanding sarcasm and figures of speech (see Supplemental Session 10) because adolescents often joke around with one another when hanging out.

Group leaders should discuss the issue of mingling with group members, and point out that while they will be hanging out with friends, they should also be comfortable with mingling with others at the dance. They should let group members know that there will be times when friends will be dancing and the group member may be left alone for awhile. Group leaders should highlight that it is not appropriate to follow friends around the entire evening, especially if the friends are dancing with others, and should explain that they may spend most of the evening with a few friends, but there will be times when the friends will not be available to hang out. This can be a stressful time for any adolescent, especially adolescents with AS. Group leaders should facilitate a discussion of what they should do if left alone at the dance: get some refreshments, briefly say hello and chat with an acquaintance if one is nearby, or ask someone to dance.

Asking someone to dance

Group leaders should facilitate a discussion regarding how to ask someone to dance. They should point out that generally it is a good idea to ask someone who is at least an acquaintance; you generally do not ask someone that you do not know at all or who does not know you at all. Group leaders should also highlight that it is generally a good idea to approach someone when they are standing or sitting alone as opposed to approaching someone who is with a large group. Adolescents are usually worried about being embarrassed if the other person says "no" to their request; thus, if the other person is not in a large group, it reduces the potential audience.

Group leaders should remind group members to use their chit-chat and conversational skills to strike up a conversation with the person they are interested in asking to dance. Given that the event is a dance, it is not necessary to engage in a long dialogue prior to asking the person to dance. Group members could simply say hello and ask how the other person is enjoying the dance and then ask the person to dance. For example, group members could say something such as, "Hi, how are you doing tonight? Are you having a good time?" Group leaders should explain that group members should wait for the person's response to these initial chit-chat questions to get a sense of how the person is responding to being approached. They should highlight that it is important to pay attention to the other person's social cues during the initial chit-chat because it can give you an idea of how the person is going to respond to your request to dance.

Group leaders should ask group members what social cues would indicate the other person is enjoying chit-chatting with you, such as smiling at you, answering your questions, asking you questions, and standing close to you. They should also ask group members what social cues would indicate the person is trying to "brush you off" or is not interested in chit-chatting with you, such as:

- abruptly ending the conversation
- responding very briefly to your questions
- not asking you any questions
- appearing bored or disinterested
- backing away from you
- not making eye contact with you.

If the person does not seem to be interested in chit-chatting with you, you should just end the conversation appropriately and not ask the person to dance. For example, you could say, "Well, it was nice talking with you. Hope you enjoy the rest of the dance." If the person does seem to be interested in chit-chatting with you, you can ask the person to dance. For example, you could simply say, "Would you like to dance?"

Next, group leaders should talk with group members about how to respond to the person's response to the request to dance. If the person says yes, then you should obviously walk with the person to the dance floor and you should walk next to the person. If the person says no, you should still end the conversation appropriately saying something such as, "That's OK. It was still nice talking with you—see you later." Group leaders should talk with group members about the fact that many times people will not say "no," but will instead state a reason why they cannot dance. In these instances it is sometimes hard to tell if the person really has a reason they cannot dance at that particular moment or if they are trying to "brush you off" without hurting your feelings. For example, instead of saying "no" someone might say, "Maybe later" or "I'm waiting for my friend right now." Generally, these types of responses mean the person does not want to dance with you. As a rule of thumb, if you are unsure, only ask one more time during the dance and if they continue to respond in the same way, then it is usually safe to assume that they do not want to dance with you.

Introduce "School Dance Card" game

Group leaders should explain to group members that they will now have the opportunity to practice the social skills they will need when attending a school dance (see below).

"School Dance Card" game

Materials

- Cards with school dance scenarios written on them

Directions

Prior to the start of group, group leaders should make cards with school dance scenarios written on them. See below for school dance scenario cards. One at a time, group members will select a card from the pile, read the scenario to the group, and then provide a "solution" to the school dance scenario or question. If the group member who drew the card needs help, other group members can provide suggestions and group leaders should facilitate the activity.

"School Dance Card" game scenarios

1. You arrive at the dance with a couple of friends. What should you do now that you have arrived?

2. Your friends are all not around at the moment. You realize that you are alone. What should you do?

3. You would like to ask someone to dance with you. How will you know who to ask and when to ask?

4. You are chit-chatting with someone who you would like to ask to dance with you. This other person is answering your questions very briefly and is not asking you any questions. What could this mean? What should you do or say?

5. You decide to ask someone to dance with you. They answered by saying, "Maybe later." What could this mean? Should you ask the person again later? How will you decide?

6. You would like to ask someone to dance. You see someone that you know and you approach him or her. What should you do or say?

7. You are chit-chatting with someone that you would like to ask to dance with you. This other person is smiling at you, asking you questions, and is making good eye contact. Should you ask this person to dance with you? How will you decide?

8. You are planning to go to a school dance. What should you wear? How will you know what to wear?

Snack and social time

During snack time, group members should be encouraged to chit-chat with one another, practicing their "hanging out" skills. Group leaders should facilitate this social time.

Closing

At the end of the session, group members should be encouraged to appropriately tell each other goodbye and that they will see each other again next week. If there are any special upcoming occasions (e.g., birthdays, vacations, holidays), they should be encouraged to acknowledge them to one another. Distribute parent handouts to the parents and also provide parents with a copy of the teacher handout that they can share with their adolescent's teachers.

Adolescent Supplemental Session 2: School dances

PARENT HANDOUT

What we did during group today

Today we talked about appropriate social behavior when attending a school dance. We discussed issues related to a school dance such as appropriate dress, what people do at a dance, how to hang out with friends at a dance, and how to ask someone to dance. We practiced these skills by playing the "School Dance Card" game in which we picked cards with school dance scenarios on them. We worked with other group members to think of "solutions" to the school dance scenarios on the cards.

What to work on at home

At home, you can help your adolescent by presenting school dance scenarios to him or her and working with your adolescent to think of a good social response. One of the issues that often causes adolescents to be nervous about attending a school dance is asking others to dance. You can help your adolescent by working with him or her on determining who to ask to dance, chit-chat topics to start a conversation, and how to respond to the other person whether they say "yes," "no," or "maybe later."

Adolescent Supplemental Session 2: School dances

TEACHER HANDOUT

What we did in group this week

This week we talked about appropriate social behavior when attending a school dance. We discussed issues related to a school dance such as appropriate dress, what people do at a dance, how to hang out with friends at a dance, and how to ask someone to dance. We practiced these skills by playing the "School Dance Card" game in which we picked cards with school dance scenarios on them. We worked with other group members to think of "solutions" to the school dance scenarios on the cards.

What to work on at school

At school, you can remind the adolescent of upcoming school dances and talk with him or her about appropriate social behavior at a school dance. You can talk with the adolescent about issues such as what to wear, who to hang out with at the dance, and who to ask to dance. You can even roleplay some "school dance scenarios" with him or her.

Adolescent Supplemental Session 3: Interviewing skills

Aim of session

The aim of this group session is to teach group members interviewing skills for potential jobs.

Empirical basis for the skill

Adolescence is a time in which many teens seek part-time employment. Marriage and colleagues (1995) point out that individuals with AS often have difficulty obtaining employment, especially in occupations that require direct interaction with the public. Participating in a job interview is a highly social event, one that requires excellent social skills. Therefore, it is important to teach adolescents with AS interviewing skills in order to increase their ability to obtain employment. A number of social skills groups for adolescents have addressed this issue specifically (Howlin and Yates 1999; Williams 1989).

Introduce interviewing skills

Group leaders should ask group members to discuss what jobs they think they would like to pursue as teens. They should make note of these jobs and use them in the mock interviews and examples discussed in order to make the group session highly relevant for each of the group members. They should review with group members how to appropriately greet someone formally and the importance of using a good handshake and eye contact. Group leaders should facilitate a discussion with group members regarding what they think they will be asked in a job interview and appropriate responses to those questions. In addition, they should ensure that group members discuss the great importance of nonverbal behavior during an interview, such as smiling, making good eye contact, and so forth. They should highlight that even if you are highly qualified for a job, how you come across socially is often even more important in a job interview.

Group leaders should discuss with group members the importance of being very positive during an interview, highlighting for the interviewer why you are qualified for the position. Of course, you should be honest, but you should also not focus on the negative. It is also important to answer all of the interviewer's questions and to not respond "I don't know" to questions—you should think of something appropriate to say. Even if the interviewer has asked you a question to which you do not know the answer, you should say something about how you would find the answer. For example, you could say something such as, "To be honest, I'm actually not sure about that but here's what I would do to find out…"

Group leaders should also discuss with group members how to appropriately leave the interview. You should continue to use good, positive nonverbal communication all the way through the end of the interview. You will want to express appreciation for the opportunity to interview and that you are looking forward to hearing from the interviewer about the position. For example, you could say something such as, "Thank you very much for the opportunity to interview with you. I look forward to hearing from you soon." While saying something like this, it is appropriate to shake the interviewer's hand again as you leave.

Introduce mock interviews and job hunting activity

Each group member will have the opportunity to participate in a mock job interview with a group leader for a job that the teen has expressed interest in obtaining. Group leaders may want to find other adults to act as group leaders for this session in order for each group member to have the opportunity to participate in a one-on-one mock interview. While some group members are participating in mock interviews, the rest of the group members will discuss job hunting skills with a group leader.

Mock interviews

Group leaders should set up the mock interview rooms to mimic an office setting. They should briefly review with the group member the job for which the group member will be interviewing (i.e., landscaping, office work, etc.) and may also briefly review some of the basics of interviewing (i.e., appropriate greetings, good nonverbal communication, staying positive, etc.). They should then start the interview with the group member. They should have group members wait outside the door and then call the group member in for the interview. If a group member struggles at some point during the interview or does something inappropriate, a "time out" can be taken in which the group leader provides some coaching and then that particular portion of the mock interview is roleplayed again to ensure the group member understands and can demonstrate the appropriate skill.

Mock interview key points

- Be sure the adolescent greets you appropriately—smiles, introduces self, firm handshake.

- Check for appropriate chit-chat while you walk with the adolescent into the "office."

- Make sure the adolescent provides an appropriate response to all questions posed.

- Be sure the adolescent stays positive and is not negative.

- Check for good nonverbal communication throughout the interview.

- Make sure the adolescent leaves the interview well—saying thank you, looking forward to hearing about the position, firm handshake, smiling.

Mock interview question ideas

These are simply question ideas. Group leaders are encouraged to personalize the mock interview questions to the particular group member and his or her specific job interest.

- Why are you interested in this position?

- What qualifications do you have to perform this job?

- Are you seeking part-time or full-time employment?

- How many hours per week would you be available to work?

- What transportation will you rely on?

- How will you be able to manage going to school and working for us?

- How long would you like to work for us? Are you looking for a temporary position such as only for the summer or would you like a more permanent position?

- How much money are you expecting to make in this position?

- Tell me about your personality.

- What do you like to do in your spare time?

Job hunting activity

While some group members are participating in the mock interviews, the other group members should meet with a group leader to discuss how to "job hunt." The group leader should discuss with group members how to go about finding a job (i.e., looking in the newspaper, asking friends and family if they know of any positions, talking with a school counselor, etc.). The group leader should also talk with group members about who they can use as a resource to create a résumé. Group members should be encouraged to talk with their school guidance counselors, teachers, and parents about how to create a résumé.

The group leader should discuss with group members how to make the initial phone call regarding a position. He or she should assure that certain issues are addressed: state your name, the position you are interested in, how you found out about the open position, inquire about obtaining an application, and so forth. Group members can roleplay a few mock phone calls with the group leader, time permitting. The group leader should also discuss with group members that if they do not hear back from a company regarding the position for which they applied, they should call to follow up. For example, group members could say something such as, "Hello, I am _____. I applied about a week ago for the _____ position and I was calling to check and see if the position has been filled yet."

The group leader should practice these skills with group members as time permits. The group leader should provide group members with some tips such as speaking clearly on the phone, not talking too fast, and smiling while talking to come across as pleasant over the phone. The group leader should highlight that it is important for group members to pay attention to their tones of voice on the phone because this is the only social cue the other person has; group members should be sure that they are using a pleasant tone of voice.

Snack and social time

During snack time, group members should again be encouraged to chit-chat with one another, practicing their "hanging out" skills. "Hanging out" is an important skill of adolescence and group leaders should encourage group members to interact in a relaxed manner with each other.

Closing

At the end of the session, group members should be encouraged to appropriately tell each other goodbye and that they will see each other again next week. If there are any special upcoming occasions (e.g., birthdays, vacations, holidays), they should be encouraged to acknowledge them to one another. Distribute parent handouts to the parents and also provide parents with a copy of the teacher handout that they can share with their adolescent's teachers.

Adolescent Supplemental Session 3: Interviewing skills

PARENT HANDOUT

What we did during group today

Today we talked about job hunting skills and interviewing skills. We discussed how to find a potential job and appropriate social behavior during a job interview. We learned that it is very important to be positive during an interview and to use good nonverbal communication such as smiling, making eye contact, and having a firm handshake. We had the opportunity to practice our interviewing skills in a mock job interview with a group leader.

What to work on at home

At home, you can help your adolescent by helping him or her think about what types of jobs are of interest. Then, you can help your adolescent think of potential places of employment and how to find out if they have any openings. You can also encourage him or her to talk with the school guidance counselor about finding employment and creating a résumé. You can even practice with your adolescent by engaging in a mock interview and providing coaching as needed.

Adolescent Supplemental Session 3: Interviewing skills

TEACHER HANDOUT

What we did in group this week

This week we talked about job hunting skills and interviewing skills. We discussed how to find a potential job and appropriate social behavior during a job interview. We learned that it is very important to be positive during an interview and to use good nonverbal communication such as smiling, making eye contact, and having a firm handshake. We had the opportunity to practice our interviewing skills in a mock job interview with a group leader.

What to work on at school

You can talk with the adolescent about the resources available at school to help him or her find employment and create a résumé. If appropriate, you can help the adolescent set up a time to meet with the school guidance counselor regarding vocational issues. You can also help the adolescent think about the skills he or she has and what potential jobs would be appropriate. You can even participate in a mock job interview with the adolescent and provide coaching as needed.

PART III

FURTHER READING

Appendix: Theoretical Background to this Resource

Group interventions related to autism spectrum disorders

This appendix is included in order to give the reader access to the studies that were reviewed to create this resource. The following is a summary of the studies that were used to inform the development of the curriculum outlined here.

Mesibov (1984)

One of the first studies examining the effectiveness of social skills groups for individuals on the autism spectrum was conducted by Mesibov (1984). Mesibov's group targeted improving how to: meet other people, stay on the topic of conversation, ask questions, pay attention, and express feelings and emotions appropriately. More broadly, the group aimed to promote positive peer interactions in a supportive environment. The teaching techniques utilized in this group were modeling, coaching, and roleplaying. The 15-member group met weekly for 10 to 12 weeks and each session lasted 60 minutes. Prior to the start of group, each client met individually with a staff member for 30 minutes to practice the major lesson for the day in order to allow an opportunity for one-on-one teaching of skills. The group sessions were broken down into four parts: group discussion, listening and talking, roleplaying, and appreciation of humor.

The group discussion portion of the session occurred while all group members had a snack due to the time of the evening (5:30 pm) and because food is often a strong motivator for individuals on the autism spectrum. The discussion during snack was not as highly structured as the rest of the group and topics of conversation often included what members had done during the week, future plans, common interests among members, and any concerns group members might have.

During the listening and talking portion of the group, members were paired with a staff member and practiced "attending skills, the expression and identification of emotions, and two person interactive activities" (Mesibov 1984, p.399). In the pairs, the staff member and client discussed an issue and then shared what was said with the other group members. This portion of the group also focused on discussing emotions and acting out scenes in which group members had to guess the emotion of the actor.

The roleplaying portion of the group was a key component for teaching specific social skills to the group members. The specific skill for that session was practiced in a one-on-one setting prior to the start of the group session. Then the specific skill was first identified, explained, and then practiced using roleplays, initially with staff members and then with other clients in the group. The execution of the social skill was broken down into specific steps and then members practiced these skills while receiving feedback from staff members and other participants. Examples of skills taught included greetings, conversational skills, going to a restaurant, meeting others in social settings (i.e., at a party), and going on a trip. The group participated in these activities in the weeks following the teaching of the specific skill.

The appreciation of humor portion of the group was accomplished by having a "joke time" at the end of each group session. This portion of the group was included because humor is often a difficult skill for individuals with an autism spectrum disorder (ASD) to display, and humor is often very subtle and hard to pick up on for them. Initially this portion of the group was challenging for the clients but they soon expressed that this was their favorite part of group. The jokes generally consisted of simple riddles and "knock-knock" jokes that both staff and clients shared with the group.

Effectiveness of the group was assessed by self-report measures, roleplayed social situations, and skill measures. Results suggested that the group was able to provide the clients with positive peer social interactions in a supportive context. In addition, both the clients and parents demonstrated great enthusiasm about the group and parents reported seeing improvements in areas such as eye contact, conversational skills, and responding appropriately to strangers. The roleplays that were used to evaluate effectiveness of the group indicated that the group members showed improvement in initiating and sustaining one-on-one conversations. Additionally, the self-concept measures suggested that the clients' self-perceptions had improved through participating in the group. While some improvements were noted, the procedure unfortunately did not include standardized, objective pre and post test measures. Nevertheless, one of the major contributions of this study was the effectiveness of using roleplays with individuals on the autism spectrum. Given the pretend nature of roleplays, some question existed regarding the potential usefulness of roleplays with individuals on the autism spectrum, but this study demonstrated that roleplays are generally an effective and concrete way to teach social skills to clients with an ASD.

Williams (1989)

Another study that examined group-based social skills interventions for individuals on the autism spectrum was conducted by Williams (1989). The group in this study included ten group participants and the duration of the group was four years. The group met once per week during the school year. The sessions were 45 minutes in length and took place immediately after school. The types of activities used in the group included recreational games, roleplay exercises, and modeling. Group participants were reinforced for demonstrating good social skills, and videotape and direct verbal feedback were utilized for social interactions that were unsuccessful. Williams (1989) highlighted that the group strived to teach "children how to think, not what to think" in social interactions (p.147). The initial sessions included cooperative games. The group leaders found that the children were not necessarily able to organize activities for themselves that would include all group members, but the children were able to participate more fully when clear rules were put in place regarding the games.

The group also included the use of roleplays. Like Mesibov (1984), the staff of the Williams (1989) study wondered if the children would be able to pretend and participate in roleplays. Therefore, the next sessions explored pretend activities. Williams found that the children were not only able to pretend well, they were able to engage in fairly complex roleplays with few difficulties. As the group members became more comfortable with the roleplays, the staff began introducing concepts such as using appropriate eye contact with the other members in the roleplay. The staff created some roleplays to focus on specific social situations such as meeting someone, asking for tickets, asking for help finding groceries, and asking for help in a library. These roleplays were videotaped and the staff reported that the children enjoyed seeing the video roleplays of their attempts at social interactions. The staff also found that when they asked the children to roleplay emotions and had the other group members guess the emotion portrayed, the members were able to roleplay strong, distinct emotions much better than more subtle emotions.

The next focus of the group was conversational skills. The staff noticed that the most difficult conversational skill for the group members was giving nonverbal indicators of interest in the other person. Despite the initial difficulty with conversational skills, the staff noted that by the end of this sequence, the children were able to demonstrate both good and poor social skills in a conversational context.

Next, the group sessions concentrated on the use of tone of voice. The staff first used voice exercises to help the members become more aware of voice and intonation by asking them to vary their tone of voice across different words. Next, nonsense words were used and the group members were asked to say these words with a voice intonation indicating a question or surprise. Conversational skills were integrated into this section of the group sessions and the children were found to display notable difficulties in knowing what to say in a conversation and how to respond to their conversational partners' comments.

Issues such as how to say goodbye and discovering what others are interested in were also covered in the group sessions. The staff continued to point out issues such as using appropriate amounts of eye contact and they assisted group members in finding their own conversational strategies as opposed to being taught "rules" of conversations.

The group also covered how to convey empathy to others so that they do not appear rude or uncaring about others. Poor social skills were modeled and the group members were asked to identify the problems in the model and then roleplay how the scenario should have proceeded. Skills such as acknowledging others when spoken to were a focus of some of the roleplays.

Additionally, the group examined situations that can cause an anger response, such as tripping over someone else's belongings or having one's toe stepped on. The staff found that these roleplays ignited fierce anger responses from the group members and even though they were eventually able to respond somewhat appropriately to these types of situations, these skills did not generalize well. The staff noted that the central problem seemed to be that in this portion of the group, the members were not able to take the other person's point of view, a common theory of mind problem in individuals who have an ASD.

Another issue addressed in group was helping group members be more flexible in their responses to others. They were encouraged to think of a number of responses to specific situations, instead of having simply one response to each situation.

Toward the end of the group sequence, the focus turned toward helping those who would be leaving the school system to improve their interviewing skills. During these exercises, staff noticed that many group members had poor listening skills, which they addressed by teaching the group members how to play "20 Questions." The staff also had group members select a topic of interest, present it to the group, and then answer questions.

In general, the staff became aware that session topics took far more time to cover in their group than predicted. In addition, Williams encouraged others to develop techniques that address generalization of skills in individuals on the autism spectrum.

In order to evaluate the effectiveness of the group, Williams (1989) utilized the social behavior questionnaire developed by Spence (1980), a measure that describes deficits in social skills. This measure was administered at the start of the group and at the conclusion of the group four years later. The measures were completed by a staff member who knew the child well. Due to a staff member retiring, only 7 of the 10 children had two complete sets of questionnaires. The results indicated that all seven group members showed improvements. A more informal approach to evaluation of the group was also used. Group members were asked what they would like to work on most at the beginning of the group sequence. The group members indicated that they would like to know how to make friends, and at the end of the group 8 of the 10 group members had at least one friend. Overall, the results demonstrated improved peer relationships, better use of appropriate facial expressions, and higher frequency of participation in a peer group setting.

Williams pointed out that the study lacked a control group and therefore it cannot be concluded that the improvements produced are greater than those that would have occurred due to maturation alone. Williams also noted that even if a control group had been used, it would still not be clear if the improvements were related specifically to social skills training or to the group members meeting as a group in general. Nonetheless, the group did seem to be beneficial to those individuals who participated.

Marriage, Gordon, and Brand (1995)

Another study that examined the effectiveness of social skills groups for individuals on the autism spectrum specifically focused on boys with Asperger's Syndrome (AS) (Marriage *et al.* 1995). The group included boys who ranged in age from 8 to 12 years and met weekly for 14 sessions. The sessions were divided into two phases, the first phase lasted for eight weeks and each group session was two hours in duration; eight boys attended this first phase. The second phase met for six weeks and met for one and a half hours, and six of the eight boys returned. The authors noted that the two most socially skilled boys were the two who did not return for the second phase. Included in the group structure was a snack time which fell in the middle of the group session.

The staff focused on moving from relatively simple skills to more advanced social skills. The skills chosen to be addressed in the group were based upon deficits covered in the literature and the staff's knowledge of the boys, as well as from the staff's experience. The staff were also very aware of the difficulty children with AS have with generalizing the skills they learn and, in an effort to address this issue, they conducted the groups in four different sites and rotated the staff member who acted as the group leader. A curriculum sheet was given to the parents of the group members in order to keep them informed about the skills their children were learning in group. In the first phase of the group, the children were given a homework sheet which was collected and discussed in the next group meeting, and in the second phase of the group, no homework sheets were used. In addition, the parents of the group members met informally while their children were in group and discussed how they were coping with challenges and other pertinent issues.

The group staff used a number of techniques during the group to teach social skills. All group sessions began with a warm-up exercise that served to provide movement and also acted to help group members learn each other's names, and the group staff reported finding these exercises useful. Another technique used was roleplays in which some group members acted out particular social interactions and other group members evaluated their demonstration of the target social skills. The group members watching the roleplay were assigned to watch for certain skills such as eye contact and prompt cards were used to remind those watching of what they should be looking for. The staff noticed that once one roleplay had been done, subsequent roleplays tended to use the same topic of conversation and the staff were particularly struck by this rigidity. In addition, the staff indicated that they thought the group members learned from the roleplays but progress was slower than expected.

An additional technique used was videotaping and viewing exercises. The staff noted that the effectiveness of this technique appeared to be marginal because the group members seemed more focused on competing to be the cameraman than on the task at hand. Additionally, although the group members attended to the video when it was being shown, they were not able to identify emotions, individuals' perceptions, and specific social skills very well, and the group members continued to have similar difficulties when they were shown movie clips. As a result, the staff reduced the use of video in the second phase of the group sessions.

Games were also used and a "show and tell" game seemed to be particularly useful. In this game, a group member would discuss a topic of interest for five minutes and the presenter was to watch for cues that the audience might be getting bored, a task that proved difficult for most group members. A number of other exercises were used such as creating collages from magazines for different emotions and working as a team on a cooking task. The staff noticed that the group members seemed to do better with these very concrete activities as opposed to more abstract or less "hands on" activities.

At the end of all group sessions, in the first phase of the group, each group member was given a homework sheet with one to three tasks listed on it that they were to complete before the next group meeting. Examples included figuring out the emotions of parents and siblings, interviewing family members about their favorite activities, and noticing what people talk about when in conversation. The group members were required to provide written answers and at group the following week, they discussed their experiences in a small group format. The staff reported that these homework activities seemed to be helpful in that they highlighted for parents and therapists the specific struggles the group members faced more concretely and assisted them in helping the group members individually.

The parents of group members reported that they found meeting weekly to be very helpful to them. They shared information about AS and provided advice and moral support for one another.

In order to evaluate the effectiveness of the group, questionnaires addressing five social skill areas (holding a conversation with peers, holding a conversation with adults, behaving correctly in public, joining activities with peers, and responding appropriately to criticism) were given to parents prior to the first group session and after the eighth group session, which was the end of the first phase. Results indicated that there were very few differences between the pre and post group ratings. The parents, however, made comments on the rating sheets about particular areas of improvement that they noticed in their children such as: better eye contact, better ability to verbalize feelings, more likely to initiate social contact, and being more aware of others' interests. In addition, staff indicated that they saw progress in all the group members, especially with regard to self confidence and learning some concrete social skills. Interestingly, however, reports from the group members' parents and their respective schools indicated that the skills they seemed to have gained in the group did not generalize well to other community settings, such as the home and school settings. Given this information, Marriage and colleagues suggested conducting the social skills groups in the school setting in order to promote generalization to interactions with classmates. Lastly, Marriage and colleagues pointed out that the parents of group members suggested to them that it would be helpful if the group members were able to invite each other over to their homes to play, so that their friendships could be continued outside of the group setting.

Ozonoff and Miller (1995)

Ozonoff and Miller (1995) also examined the effectiveness of social skills groups for adolescents on the autism spectrum. The group members were five boys of normal IQ, and matched controls were also included in the study. The control group included four boys matched on age, IQ, and severity of autism and they received no treatment. The treatment group met on a weekly basis for 90 minutes over a 14-week period.

Each group session started with snack time during which group members were encouraged to interact with one another and staff members to practice their conversational skills. The importance of possessing good social skills was discussed and each particular skill was presented in a simple, concrete fashion and was broken down into its components. Staff modeled the target skill for the session by roleplaying it for the group and then group members were videotaped roleplaying the skill while being coached by staff. Then the videotaped segments were watched and group members were given both positive reinforcement and constructive feedback about their roleplays. The session ended with a game such as Bingo or Wheel of Fortune.

The staff divided the sessions into two units, each lasting seven weeks. The first unit addressed topics such as initiating, maintaining, and ending conversations, interpreting and displaying nonverbal communication, listening skills, giving compliments, sharing, and showing interest in others.

The second unit focused more specifically on theory of mind activities and developing perspective-taking abilities. This specific focus was chosen due to the known difficulties individuals on the autism spectrum have with understanding others' perspectives and points of view. In order to make the notion of perspective-taking more concrete, the topic was introduced by having group members lead a blindfolded staff member through a maze. This activity required group members to take on the physical perspective of the staff member and understand that the staff member could not see what they could see. Next, the staff introduced that not only can people's physical perspectives differ, but also their cognitive perspectives can be different, and emphasized the idea that "perception influences knowledge" (Ozonoff and Miller 1995, p.422). Roleplays were used to teach how one person can know something that another does not. The boys in the treatment group were able to master this task within two sessions. The group then focused on predicting what someone thinks another person thinks.

The group also aimed to help the group members realize that social interactions can be enjoyable and fun and they did this by alternating traditional group sessions with field trips into the community such as to restaurants and malls. During these outings, the group members were encouraged to have fun and also to work on social skills such as starting conversations with others seated with them at the restaurant. Following the outing, group members were given feedback about their social skills. In addition, the games at the end of the more traditional group sessions were used to demonstrate that social interactions can be enjoyable and social skills were integrated into these games as well.

Ozonoff and Miller strove to evaluate the effectiveness of their social skills group both by including a control group and by administering particular tests before and after group. Prior to the start of group, all nine boys were given multiple theory of mind tests and these tests were readministered at the conclusion of the group, four and a half months later. Parents and teachers were asked to rate how often their child displayed social skills that were included on the Social Skills Rating System (SSRS) both before and after the group.

With regard to the group members' performance on the theory of mind tests, the treatment and no treatment groups were not statistically different prior to the start of group. When the participants were tested post treatment, the treatment group had improved and the no treatment group remained the same. More specifically, improvements in the treatment group's performance were on the false belief tasks. When the teacher and parent SSRS scores were examined, the results indicated that the treatment and no treatment groups were not statistically different at pre or post testing. Thus, although the treatment group showed significant improvements in theory of mind tasks, general social skills did not seem to improve as a result of participating in the group. Ozonoff and Miller argued that the results of the SSRS may not have necessarily indicated a lack of generalization of skills but may have instead highlighted that the SSRS did not specifically assess perspective-taking skills, the main focus of the group treatment intervention. Nevertheless, Ozonoff and Miller demonstrated that theory of mind and perspective-taking skills can be effectively taught to individuals with an ASD.

Howlin and Yates (1999)

Howlin and Yates (1999) conducted a social skills group for adults with a diagnosis of autism or AS. Ten males participated in the year-long group and ranged in age from 19 to 44. The group focused on improving the group members' conversational skills as well as their level of independence in work and home settings. The group met once per month for two and a half hours for 12 sessions. The first portion of each session allowed group members to share any important events that occurred since the last meeting and each session followed a specified agenda that focused on the skill(s) to be covered. Social skills that were covered included initiating and maintaining conversations, communicating with friends and strangers, assertiveness skills, problem solving, job interviewing skills, understanding body language, and coping with stressful situations. Teaching techniques that were utilized included roleplays, team activities, structured games, and feedback from videotapes taken during group sessions. In addition, real-life examples from the lives of the group members were used as teaching opportunities.

Howlin and Yates examined the effectiveness of their group intervention in a few ways. First, they asked both the group members and their respective families to complete a checklist that addressed social skills that may have improved since the start of the group. Results indicated that all the families who responded reported improvements in conversational and social skills, physical appearance, self-confidence, and independence skills. Most families also acknowledged improvements in problem-solving skills and friendship skills. The vast majority of the group members reported feeling improvements in their conversational skills, their abilities to interpret emotions, their ability to relate to others, their problem-solving skills, and their decision-making skills. All of the group members indicated that the group was helpful in that it provided them with the opportunity to meet and interact with others who were experiencing similar difficulties.

In addition, Howlin and Yates evaluated the effectiveness of the group intervention by videotaping social situations both at the start of group and at the end of group. Each group member was required to participate in two structured social activities, chatting with someone at a wedding party and being interviewed for a job. The results indicated that the amount of speech did not change between pre and post testing but there were differences in content. Speech used to initiate and maintain conversations increased, the group members gave more appropriate responses to questions, and the group members made fewer inappropriate statements or comments.

Howlin and Yates recognized the methodological problems with their study in that it did not include a control group and the methods of evaluating effectiveness were subjective in nature. Howlin and Yates did, however, point out that some improvements were seen in the group members' social skills. More qualitatively, they found that by the end of the group, several group members were able to attain higher levels of employment and/or independent living arrangements. Howlin and Yates also highlighted the difficulty with the generalization of social skills taught in group. They reported that while the group members were eventually able to demonstrate adequate social skills within the group setting, they continued to receive reports that they were behaving in socially inappropriate ways outside of the group setting. Lastly, Howlin and Yates highlighted the importance of recognizing comorbid mental health issues and treating those issues in a separate setting from group. They advocated individual treatment for group members who are experiencing other significant difficulties because comorbid mental health issues simply cannot be adequately addressed in a group designed to address general difficulties associated with having autism or AS.

Barnhill, Cook, Tebbenkamp, and Myles (2002)

Barnhill and colleagues (2002) conducted a social skills group with eight adolescent boys with AS and related pervasive developmental delays. The group met weekly for one hour of social skills instruction over a period of eight weeks at a local university classroom. The first four weeks of the program focused on paralanguage, including recognizing emotion by tone of voice, learning the meaning of sounds (i.e., "mmm"), exploring the implied meanings of rate of speech, and learning how emphasized words can change the meaning of a statement. The last four weeks of the program aimed to improve group members' ability to identify and respond to others' facial expressions. Activities focusing on facial expressions included viewing videos without sound to identify emotions, using mirrors to mimic various facial expressions, and varying the intensities of facial expressions. Interventions used throughout the program included roleplays, modeling, and reinforcing feedback.

After each session, the adolescents engaged in a recreational activity within the community for an additional two to three hours. Group staff reminded the group members to be aware of nonverbal forms of communication and the members were reinforced for appropriately attending to the nonverbal expressions of peers. The recreational outings included activities such as going to a movie, dining at a restaurant, and bowling.

In order to assess the effectiveness of the social skills group, the *Diagnostic Analysis of Nonverbal Accuracy 2* (DANVA2) was administered pre and post treatment to evaluate group members' abilities to recognize emotions in facial expressions and tone of voice. In addition, a survey was developed by the authors and was administered to parents at the last social skills group session, asking them to anonymously comment on their children's experiences with the group and what skills the group should cover in the future. Group members were given a similar survey as well.

The results of the study indicated that the majority of the group members (6 of the 8) showed improvements on at least one subtest of the DANVA2. With regard to the parent surveys, all reported that they wanted their children to continue in the social skills group, and 75% reported that their child had made friends within the group. Similarly, 87% of the group members reported that they made friends with other group members. The majority of the parents reported that they would like to see phone skills, accepting criticism, and starting and maintaining conversations targeted in future group sessions. The majority of the group members indicated that they would like to learn how to talk to the opposite sex, accept criticism, talk on the phone, deal with fear and anxiety, and deal with bullies.

Cragar and Horvath (2003)

Cragar and Horvath (2003) reported on a case study of a ten-year-old boy, Billy, who was diagnosed with AS and participated in a group-based social skills program. The group was designed for children between 10 and 12 years of age and met weekly for 1 hour and 50 minutes for a total of ten sessions. Interestingly, the six group members were not all diagnosed with AS; in fact, the children had diagnoses such as ADHD and social anxiety. Cragar and Horvath described the group curriculum as being behaviorally based and as using concepts such as direct instruction, modeling, roleplaying, discussion, and homework assignments.

The group addressed a number of topics including cooperation, perspective-taking, conversational skills, complimenting, anger management, group entry, and appropriate complaints. Specific awards were given to group members each week such as Most Improved or Most Valuable Member. An individualized "report card" was created for each group member that addressed both negative and positive behaviors and their progress was charted on these report cards.

Another component to this group involved two parent meetings in which parents were made aware of the skills their children were learning and how to reinforce these concepts in the home setting. In addition, the staff shared behavioral management strategies used in group and how parents could adapt these strategies to the home setting.

With regard to assessing Billy's improvements, both qualitative and quantitative approaches were used. Qualitatively, the staff noticed that Billy was able to learn not to interrupt, to pick up on nonverbal cues to stop talking, and during one session was able to take another group member's perspective. At home, Billy's parents reported that he was able to interrupt less, his phone skills improved, and he was starting to play with other children at recess. Quantitatively, Billy measurably decreased his interrupting and disrespectful behaviors and once the home report card was used, his negative behaviors measurably decreased as well. Billy's mother completed the Social Skills Rating Scale (SSRS) at pre and post treatment times and these results did not indicate a significant change in Billy's social skills.

The staff followed up with Billy nine months after the treatment group ended and again, both qualitative and quantitative improvements were examined. Billy's parents reported that he continued to show improvements in initiating peer contact, recognizing his emotions, and interrupting less at school. Billy's parents also indicated that he continued to have great difficulty with perspective-taking and also continued to make inappropriate comments in various social settings. With regard to quantitative improvements, Billy's mother completed another SSRS nine months after treatment ended and Billy's scores then fell in the average range. Thus, although Billy's mother rated his social skills as impaired both before and immediately after treatment, nine months later he scored in the average range, suggesting that benefits of treatment may not be immediately measurable.

Heitzman-Powell (2003)

Heitzman-Powell (2003) examined the effectiveness of a social skills group designed for children with AS, high-functioning autism, and pervasive developmental disorder– not otherwise specified. All children who participated were of at least average intelligence, had age-appropriate verbal abilities, and were between five and eight years old. The social skills instruction occurred in pairs in the children's homes once per week for two hours over the course of six months. Eight children participated in the group and formed four pairs. Heitzman-Powell described the intervention program as a "low-intensity social-interaction training package." The purpose of the intervention being in the home setting was to increase generalizability.

Four skills were specifically targeted in this program: response to name, compliance, initiating conversations, and maintaining conversations. The activities used to teach these skills were based on parent reports of what their respective children enjoyed, such as coloring or playing with toys. The children were able to choose the activity for each session and tangible reinforcers were used to promote skill learning. At the end of each session the reinforcers could be exchanged for a larger reward.

In order to assess the effectiveness of the program, a number of measures were used. Videotaped behavioral measures were completed pretreatment and at three other times throughout the duration of the group, which consisted of standardized roleplay scenarios designed to assess the targeted skill areas. In addition, homework was a component of the program. Parents were instructed to record the number of minutes per night they worked on the targeted social skill with their children. Teachers also were asked to observe the children and record daily the social skills that the children were able to demonstrate in the school setting. If the child was able to display good social skills at school, the child would receive a reward at home. Lastly, a consumer satisfaction survey was given both pre and post treatment.

Results indicated that the largest improvements were seen in the most trained skills. Interestingly, however, the findings showed that even when "component skills" such as eye contact and head turn were mastered in one skill area (i.e., response to name), these component skills did not seem to generalize to other skill areas (i.e., compliance). This result suggested that component skills need to be trained across multiple settings and scenarios to increase skill generalization. With regard to the effectiveness of the homework component of the program, homework seemed to have large positive effects on group member behavior for some children but due to problems with missing data, conclusions could not be made about the effectiveness of homework as a whole. With regard to the social skills that the children were able to learn, little consistency was found between parent and teacher reports and the videotaped behavioral measures. The results of the videotaped behavioral measures indicated, however, that improvements were found for most group members in responding to name and compliance, but not as many gains were found in initiating and maintaining conversations. Interestingly, although the consumer satisfaction surveys demonstrated overall satisfaction with the training program, no clinically significant changes were found in the parent and teacher measures. In fact, all children were able to earn rewards for demonstrating social skills at school and all teachers reported that the program seemed to positively influence the children's behaviors, yet the teacher daily checklist data did not support these findings.

Nevertheless, skill gains were found in the videotaped behavioral measures and parents and teachers alike reported finding the program beneficial. Heitzman-Powell discussed the logistical difficulties of conducting in-home social skills training and highlighted that there were often distracting stimuli present in the home that may have interfered with the children being able to attend to the training program.

Provencal (2003)

Provencal (2003) examined the effectiveness of a social skills training program for adolescents with ASD. This study included a treatment and a "treatment as usual" control group. The treatment group had ten group members who participated in the social skills training program. The "treatment as usual" control group included nine participants who received services as usual through their local school districts and communities but who did not participate in the social skills training program. All participants were between 12 and 16 years of age. The social skills training program met once per week over the course of eight months for 90-minute sessions. The group strove to teach specific social skills to the adolescents in the treatment group and to increase their positive peer relationships.

The goals of the social skills training program included giving group members the opportunity to meet others like themselves, to teach them specific social skills, to address problem-solving strategies and techniques, and to provide community outings to facilitate generalization of the skills learned. The training program was divided into two components, an adult mediated component and a peer mediated component. The adult mediated component involved instructors presenting specific social skills to the group members and then the group members practiced these skills. The peer mediated component involved a group of adolescents from within the community (such as a religious organization) who practiced social skills with the group members in a naturalistic setting in order to promote generalization of skills. The peer mediated component was not introduced until approximately five months after the start of the group. Parents of adolescents in the treatment group also met weekly with a therapist to discuss behavior management techniques and school-related issues while their teens participated in group.

Social skills that were specifically addressed within the adult mediated component of the program included: greetings, teamwork, enhancing self-awareness, identifying emotions, self-talk, interpreting social situations, perspective-taking, enhancing communication skills, initiating and maintaining relationships, problem solving, and demonstrating positive personal attributes. Group therapists presented the target skills for the session to the group members and then group members practiced these skills and received feedback about their performance. Training techniques utilized included: direct instruction, modeling, roleplays, visual supports, self-monitoring, positive reinforcement, incidental teaching, cognitive behavioral strategies, and structured games and activities. The group members also participated in community outings to practice the social skills they learned in a community setting.

The peer mediated portion of the social skills program involved training typically developing adolescents how to interact with the group members. They were instructed to be persistent if the group member did not respond, to follow their lead in an activity, to use simple language, to provide an ongoing commentary about what they were thinking and doing, to praise the group member each time he or she initiated an interaction, and to ignore odd behaviors. The activities with the typical peers included free play paired activities, roleplays to practice social skills, and crafts or group games. In addition, once per month a community outing was planned to foster generalization of interactions with same age peers.

In order to examine the effectiveness of the social skills training program, a number of measures were administered pre and post treatment to both the treatment group and the control group. The Social Skills Rating Scale-Student Form (SSRS) is a self-report measure that examines social behavior and it was given to all adolescents participating in the study. The Emotion Perception Test was also administered and involved having the adolescents match photographs of adults expressing particular emotions. The Emotion Perception Test also required the adolescents to state the emotion being expressed by the person in the photograph. In addition, the self-report version of the Behavior Assessment System for Children (BASC) was administered, and this test has four composite scores, School Maladjustment, Clinical Maladjustment, Personal Adjustment, and an overall Behavioral Symptom Index. The Friendship Interview (a semi-structured interview that examines the quality and nature of friendships) was also included as part of the battery of measures. The Children's Depression Inventory (CDI), a self-report measure, was administered to assess for symptoms of depression. The Revised Children's Manifest Anxiety Scale (RCMAS), also a self-report measure, examines symptoms of anxiety in children and adolescents.

Given that much of the research has pointed to the lack of evidence of generalization of skills learned in groups, Provencal included measures to specifically address this issue. The parent and teacher forms of the SSRS were used and this measure asked respondents to rate the frequency of certain social behaviors, such as talking to peers on the phone. In addition, the parent and teacher forms of the BASC were also used to gain general emotional and behavioral information from home and school. In addition, the Stress Index for Parents of Adolescents was given to parents to assess their level of stress related to parenting an adolescent.

Lastly, the issue of consumer satisfaction was addressed through the Behavior Interventions Rating Scale (BIRS), which measures the extent to which clients like the process and outcome of the treatment they received. Parents of adolescents in the treatment group completed the BIRS.

The results of the study indicated that the adolescents who participated in the social skills group showed improvements in some social skills, but not in others. Some symptoms of ASDs were decreased among the adolescents in the treatment group, such as having fewer one-sided conversations and a reduction in the amount of repetitive behaviors. Improvements in identification of emotion and understanding of friendships, however, were not found in the treatment group. Results from the self-report measures indicated that treatment group participants reported improved socioemotional functioning and better adaptive skills, as compared to the control group.

Parent and teacher measures indicated improvements in some social skills and in some specific emotional and behavioral functioning. Although parents did not report an overall improvement in emotional and behavioral functioning as measured by the BASC, parents and teachers reported fewer acting-out behaviors and fewer signs of withdrawal following treatment. Interestingly, although parents reported improvements in their adolescents' socioemotional functioning, parents of adolescents in the treatment group did not report decreased stress levels related to parenting their adolescents. Additionally, in contrast to adolescent self-report, parents of adolescents in the treatment group reported increased signs of anxiety following treatment. Furthermore, on a measure of consumer satisfaction, parents of adolescents in the treatment group reported minimal effectiveness and timely behavioral change.

Provencal argued that the social skills group program used in the study was effective because it resulted in the reduction of ASD symptoms and in improvement of socioemotional functioning for those adolescents who participated in the treatment. Provencal did, however, point out the small sample size and that the results should be interpreted with caution.

References

American Psychiatric Association (2000) *Diagnostic and Statistical Manual of Mental Disorders, 4th Edition, Text Revised.*Washington, DC: American Psychiatric Association.

Attwood, T. (2000) "Strategies for improving the social integration of children with Asperger syndrome." *Autism 4*, 1, 85–100.

Attwood, T. (2001) "Social skills for children and adults with Asperger's Syndrome". Conference presentation, March. Denver, CO.

Attwood, T. (2003) "Frameworks for behavioral interventions." *Child and Adolescent Psychiatric Clinics of North America 12*, 65–86.

Barnhill, G., Cook, K., Tebbenkamp, K., and Myles, B. (2002) "The effectiveness of social skills intervention targeting nonverbal communication for adolescents with Asperger Syndrome and related pervasive developmental delays." *Focus on Autism and Other Developmental Disabilities 17*, 2, 112–18.

Bloomquist, M. (1996) *Skills Training for Children with Behavior Disorders: A Parent and Therapist Guidebook.* New York: Guilford Press.

Bracken, B. A. and McCallum, R. S. (1998) *Universal Nonverbal Intelligence Test.* Itasca, Illinois: Riverside Publishing.

Broderick, C., Caswell, R., Gregory, S. Marzolini, S. and Wilson, O. (2002) "Can I join the club?" *Autism 6*, 4, 427–31.

Church, C., Alisanski, S., and Amanullah, S. (2000) "The social, behavioral, and academic experiences of children with Asperger Syndrome." *Focus on Autism and Other Developmental Disabilities 15*, 12–20.

Cragar, D. E. and Horvath, L.S. (2003) "The application of social skills training in the treatment of a child with Asperger's disorder." *Clinical Case Studies 2*, 1, 34–49.

Ehlers, S. and Gillberg, C. (1993) "The epidemiology of Asperger Syndrome. A total population study." *Journal of Child Psychology and Psychiatry 34*, 8, 1327–50.

Ehlers, S., Gillberg, C., and Wing, L. (1999) "A screening questionnaire for Asperger Syndrome and other high functioning autism spectrum disorders in school age children." *Journal of Autism and Developmental Disorders 29*, 2, 129–41.

Evers-Pasquale, W. and Sherman, M. (1975) "The reward value of peers: A variable influencing the efficacy of filmed modeling in modifying social isolation in preschoolers." *Journal of Abnormal Child Psychology 3*, 3, 179–89.

Felder, M. Asperger (2000) "Foreword." In A. Klin, F. R. Volkmar and S. S. Sparrow (eds), *Asperger Syndrome.* New York: Guilford Press.

Frith, U. (1991) "Asperger and his Syndrome." In U. Frith (ed), *Autism and Asperger Syndrome.* New York: Cambridge University Press.

Garnett, M. S. and Attwood, A. J. (1995) "The Australian Scale for Asperger's Syndrome." Paper presented at the 1995 Australian National Autism Conference, Brisbane, Australia.

Ghaziuddin, M., Tsai, L., and Ghaziuddin, N. (1992) "Brief report: A comparison of the diagnostic criteria for Asperger Syndrome." *Journal of Autism and Developmental Disorders 22*, 4, 643–9.

Gillberg, C. and Gillberg, I. C. (1989) "Asperger Syndrome—some epidemiological considerations: A research note." *Journal of Child Psychology and Psychiatry 30*, 631–8.

Gilliam, J. (2001) *Gilliam Asperger's Disorder Scale: Examiner's Manual.* Austin, Texas: PRO-ED, Inc.

REFERENCES

Gottman, J. (1977a) "The effects of a modeling film on social isolation in preschool children: A methodological investigation." *Journal of Abnormal Child Psychology 5*, 69–78.

Gottman, J. (1977b) "Toward a definition of social isolation in children." *Child Development 48*, 513–17.

Grossman, P. B. and Hughes, J. N. (1992) "Self-control interventions with internalizing disorders: A review and analysis." *School Psychology Review 21*, 2, 229–45.

Hauck, M., Fein, D., Waterhouse, L., and Feinstein, C. (1995) "Social initiations by autistic children to adults and other children." *Journal of Autism and Developmental Disorders 25*, 579–95.

Heitzman-Powell, L. S. (2003) "Social skills training for children with Asperger's syndrome, high functioning autism, and pervasive developmental disorder–not otherwise specified." *Dissertation Abstracts International 64*, 3-B, 984 (UMI No. 3082653).

Hoag, M. J. (1996) "Evaluating the effectiveness of child and adolescent group psychotherapy: A meta-analytic review." *Dissertation Abstracts International 57*, 7-B, 4709 (UMI No. 9640069).

Howlin, P. and Yates, P. (1999) "The potential effectiveness of social skills groups for adults with autism." *Autism 3*, 3, 299–307.

Kanner, L., Rodriguez, A. and Ashenden, B. (1972) "How far can autistic children go in matters of social adaptation?" *Journal of Autism and Childhood Schizophrenia 2*, 9–33.

Kiker, K. and Rosén, L. (2003) "Identification of Asperger's syndrome: A comparison of four measures." Unpublished manuscript.

Klin, A., Volkmar, F. R., and Sparrow, S. S. (eds) (2000) *Asperger syndrome.* New York: Guilford Press.

Koning, C. and Magill-Evans, J. (2001) "Social and language skills in adolescent boys with Asperger Syndrome." *Autism 5*, 1, 23–36.

Krasny, L., Williams, B., Provencal, S., and Ozonoff, S. (2003) "Social skills interventions for the autism spectrum: Essential ingredients and model curriculum." *Child and Adolescent Psychiatric Clinics of North America 12*, 107–22.

La Greca, A. and Santogrossi, D. (1980) "Social skills training with elementary school students: A behavioral group approach." *Journal of Counseling and Clinical Psychology 48*, 220–28.

Ladd, G. W. (1981) "Effectiveness of a social learning method for enhancing children's social interaction and peer acceptance." *Child Development 52*, 171–8.

Lindner, J. and Rosén, L. (in press) "Decoding of emotion through facial expression, prosody, and verbal content in children and adolescents with Asperger's syndrome." *Journal of Autism and Developmental Disorders.*

Lord, C., Risi, S., Lambrecht, L., Cook, E., Leventhal, B., DiLavore, P., *et al.* (2000) "The autism diagnostic observation schedule-generic: a standard measure of social and communication deficits associated with the spectrum of autism." *Journal of Autism and Developmental Disorders 30*, 3, 205–23.

Lord, C., Rutter, M., and Le Couteur, A. (1994) "Autism Diagnostic Interview-Revised: A revised version of a diagnostic interview for caregivers of individuals with possible pervasive developmental disorders." *Journal of Autism and Developmental Disorders 24*, 659–85.

Marriage, K. J., Gordon, V., and Brand, L. (1995) "A social skills group for boys with Asperger's syndrome." *Australian and New Zealand Journal of Psychiatry 29*, 58–62.

Mesibov, G. B. (1984) "Social skills training with verbal autistic adolescents and adults: A program model." *Journal of Autism and Developmental Disorders 14*, 4, 395–404.

Myles, B., Bock, S., and Simpson, R. (2001) *Asperger Syndrome Diagnostic Scale Examiner's Manual.* Austin, Texas: Pro-ed.

Njardvik, U., Matson, J. L., and Cherry, K. E. (1999) "A comparison of social skills in adults with autistic disorder, pervasive developmental disorder not otherwise specified, and mental retardation." *Journal of Autism and Developmental Disorders 29*, 287–95.

O'Callaghan, P., Reitman, D., Northup, J., Hupp, S., and Murphy, M. (2003) "Promoting social skills generalization with ADHD-diagnosed children in a sports setting." *Behavior Therapy 34*, 313–30.

Ozonoff, S. and Miller, J. N. (1995) "Teaching theory of mind: A new approach to social skills training for individuals with autism." *Journal of Autism and Developmental Disorders 25*, 4, 415–33.

Provencal, S. (2003) "The efficacy of a social skills training program for adolescents with autism spectrum disorders." *Dissertation Abstracts International 64*, 3-B, 1504 (UMI No. 3083611).

Putallaz, M., and Gottman, J. M. (1981) "Social skills and group acceptance." In S. R. Asher and J. M. Gottman (eds) *The Development of Children's Friendships.* New York: Cambridge University Press, pp. 116–49.

Sparrow, S. S., Ball, D., and Cicchetti, D. (1984a) *Vineland Adaptive Behavior Scales, Expanded Edition.* Circle Pines, Minnesota: American Guidance Service.

Smith, T., Magyar, C., and Arnold-Saritepe, A. (2002) "Autism spectrum disorder." In D. T. Marsh and M. A. Fristad (eds) *Handbook of Serious Emotional Disturbance in Children and Adolescents.* New York: John Wiley & Sons, Inc, pp. 131–48.

Spence, S. (1980) *Social Skills Training with Children and Adolescents.* Windsor: NFER-Nelson.

Swager, R. (1995) "Treating children who lack social skills in a pedological institute school." In H. P. J. G. van Bilsen and P. Kendall (eds) *Behavioral Approaches for Children and Adolescents.* New York: Plenum Press, pp. 95–102.

Szatmari, P., Brenner, R., and Nagy, J. (1989) "Asperger's syndrome: A review of clinical features." *Canadian Journal of Psychiatry 34*, 554–60.

Tsai, L. (2000) "Children with autism spectrum disorder: Medicine today and in the new millennium." *Focus on Autism and Other Developmental Disabilities 15*, 3, 138–45.

Wechsler, D. (2003) *Wechsler Intelligence Scale for Children-Fourth Edition.* San Antonio, Texas: The Psychological Corporation.

Weiss, M. J. and Harris, S. L. (2001) "Teaching social skills to people with autism." *Behavior Modification 25*, 5, 785–802.

Whitaker, P., Barratt, P., Joy, H., Potter, M., and Thomas, G. (1998) "Children with autism and peer group support: Using 'circles of friends'." *British Journal of Special Education 25*, 2, 60–64.

Williams, K. (1995) "Understanding the student with Asperger Syndrome: Guidelines for teachers." *Focus on Autistic Behavior 10*, 2, 9–16.

Williams, T. I. (1989) "A social skills group for autistic children." *Journal of Autism and Developmental Disorders 19*, 1, 143–55.

Wing, L. (1981) "Asperger's syndrome: A clinical account." *Psychological Medicine 11*, 115–29.

Wing, L. (1991) "The relationship between Asperger's syndrome and Kanner's autism." In U. Frith (ed.) *Autism and Asperger Syndrome.* New York: Cambridge University Press, pp. 93–121.

Wing, L. (1998) "The history of Asperger Syndrome." In E. Schopler, G. B. Mesibov and L. J. Kunce (eds) *Asperger Syndrome or High-Functioning Autism.* New York: Plenum Press, pp. 11–28.

Zwaigenbaum, L. and Szatmari, P. (1999) "Psychosocial characteristics of children with pervasive developmental disorders." In V.L. Schwean and D. Saklofske (eds) *Handbook of Psychosocial Characteristics of Exceptional Children.* New York: Plenum Press/Kluwer Academic, pp. 275–98.

Subject Index

Author Index